HAWAIIAN FOLKTALES

HAWAIIAN FOLK TALES

A COLLECTION
OF NATIVE LEGENDS

COMPILED BY
THOS. G. THRUM

MUTUAL PUBLISHING

ISBN 1-56647-166-4

Cover design by Sachi Goodwin
Cover photo courtesy Hawai'i State Archives

First Printing, June 1998
Second Printing, July 2000
Third Printing, October 2004
3 4 5 6 7 8 9

Mutual Publishing
1215 Center Street, Suite 210
Honolulu, Hawaii 96816
Ph: (808) 732-1709
Fax: (808) 734-4094
e-mail: mutual@mutualpublishing.com
www.mutualpublishing.com

Printed in Australia

PREFACE

IT is becoming more and more a matter of regret that a larger amount of systematic effort was not established in early years for the gathering and preservation of the folk-lore of the Hawaiians. The world is under lasting obligations to the late Judge Fornander, and to Dr. Rae before him, for their painstaking efforts to gather the history of this people and trace their origin and migrations; but Fornander's work only has seen the light, Dr. Rae's manuscript having been accidentally destroyed by fire.

The early attempts of Dibble and Pogue to gather history from Hawaiians themselves have preserved to native and foreign readers much that would probably otherwise have been lost. To the late Judge Andrews we are indebted for a very full grammar and dictionary of the language, as also for a valuable manuscript collection of *meles* and antiquarian literature that passed to the custody of the Board of Education.

There were native historians in those days; the newspaper articles of S. M. Kamakau, the earlier writings of David Malo, and the later contributions of G. W. Pilipo and others are but samples of a wealth of material, most of which has been lost forever to the world. From time to time Prof. W. D. Alexander,

as also C. J. Lyons, has furnished interesting extracts
from these and other hakus.

The Rev. A. O. Forbes devoted some time and
thought to the collecting of island folk-lore: and King
Kalakaua took some pains in this line also, as evidenced
by his volume of "Legends and Myths of Hawaii,"
edited by R. M. Daggett, though there is much therein
that is wholly foreign to ancient Hawaiian customs
and thought.   No one of late years had a better opportunity than Kalakaua toward collecting the *meles*, *kaaos*,
and traditions of his race; and for purposes looking
to this end there was established by law a Board of
Genealogy, which had an existence of some four years,
but nothing of permanent value resulted therefrom.

Fornander's manuscript collection of *meles*, legends,
and genealogies in the vernacular has fortunately become, by purchase, the property of the Hon. C. R.
Bishop, which insures for posterity the result of one
devoted scholar's efforts to rescue the ancient traditions
that are gradually slipping away; for the *haku meles*
(bards) of Hawaii are gone.   This fact, as also the
Hawaiian Historical Society's desire to aid and stimu-
late research into the history and traditions of this
people, strengthens the hope that some one may yet
arise to give us further insight into the legendary
folk-lore of this interesting race.

T. G. T.

Honolulu, January 1, 1907.

NOTE

IN response to repeated requests, the compiler now presents in book form the series of legends that have been made a feature of "The Hawaiian Annual" for a number of years past. The series has been enriched by the addition of several tales, the famous shark legend having been furnished for this purpose from the papers of the Hawaiian Historical Society.

The collection embraces contributions by the Rev. A. O. Forbes, Dr. N. B. Emerson, J. S. Emerson, Mrs. E. M. Nakuina, W. M. Gibson, Dr. C. M. Hyde, and others, all of whom are recognized authorities.

T. G. T.

HONOLULU, January 1, 1907.

CONTENTS

HAWAI'I'S SACRED NARRATIVES:
AN INTRODUCTION
by Glen Grant

THE sacred narratives of Hawai'i are a treasure house of my thology, legends and folk tales, representing a wealth of imagination and drama. While some of this material has attracted world wide attention, often these stories remain largely inaccessible to the *malihini*, or newcomer, as well as to many people raised in the islands. For example, those unfamiliar with tales from the past do not know that the stark peak of Olomana was once a giant thief slain by a young chief from Kaua'i, or that the so-called "Chinaman's Hat" is the tail of a monster lizard killed by the sister of Pele.

The old axiom that "truth is stranger than fiction" holds especially true in terms of Hawai'i's legendary places. Rediscovering ancient local mythology provides a compelling picture of how the islands were formed, populated and ruled by gods and chiefs. While modern English names such as "Crouching Lion," "Punchbowl" or "Paradise Park" may have colorful stories behind them, they are in no way as interesting or insightful as their original names.

The only way to reconnect with the island's sense of place, in lieu of obtaining a personal storyteller, is through the written words left by several nineteenth-century collectors of *mo'olelo*, or myth, and *ka'ao*, or tale. Fortunately for modern readers, the historians David Malo and Samuel M. Kamakau recorded the oral traditions of Hawaiians whose lives bridged the eighteenth and nineteenth centuries. Published in the Hawaiian-language newspapers of the day, these rich sources of history preserved legends of chiefs, sacred mythologies of gods and ghost-gods, infamous battles, folk tales of the common people, and the reasons behind the naming of places, stones, beaches and valleys. King Kalakaua himself added many family traditions to the stories of old in his *Legends and Myths of Hawai'i*.

Even as foreigners radically transformed the islands during the nineteenth-century, several Caucasian scholars began to record the ancient native love for an English-speaking audience. With the popularity of the Grimm brothers' first collection of "fairy tales," European and American collectors began earnestly studying ethnic groups throughout the world. In Hawai'i, this effort may have been in part motivated by the paternalistic belief that, since the native race was regarded as "passing from the scene," a nostalgic reminder of former times would preserve a people whose physical presence had vanished under the advancement of Anglo-Saxon civilization.

One of the earliest foreign scholars of Hawaiian folklore was Abraham Fornander, a Swedish theology student, who abandoned religion for life on a whaling ship. After deserting [the life of the sea] in 1844 at Honolulu, Fornander settled in the islands to become a coffee planter, surveyor, newspaper editor, inspector of schools, and a judge. Married to a Hawaiian woman, he was actively involved in native affairs and worked with young men such as Malo and Kamakau who helped him collect local lore and history. His publications *An Account of the Polynesian Race* and *Collection of Hawaiian Antiquities and Folklore* are among the most important and accurate works written in the nineteenth century. Fornander's books remain a vital resource for anyone interested in studying Hawaiian mythology, and are suggested to even the most casual reader of island history.

Among the more literary renditions of Hawaiian folklore were the publications of Thomas Thrum and William Drake Westervelt. Today their works are still the most widely read and reprinted English versions of ancient myths and legends. Brought to Hawai'i from Australia by his parents at the age of eleven in 1853, Thomas Thrum was best known as the publisher of the *Hawaiian Almanac and Annual*. He edited this compendium of useful information from 1875 to 1932. In 1888, he also co-founded the monthly magazine *Paradise of the Pacific*, later incorporated into *Honolulu Magazine*. An avid collector of Hawaiian history and lore, Thrum also had a keen interest in ancient sites, especially *heiau*, or temple. Through his efforts, over 500 temples were located and identified. His inventory became a standard reference tool for scholars, historians and archaeologists. Utilizing in part the Hawaiian language sources published by Malo and Kamakau, Thrum also helped to popularize island folk tales. Among his published works are *Hawaiian Folk Tales: A Collection of Native Legends* (1907), *Stories of the Menehune* (1910) and *More Hawaiian Folk Tales* (1923). It was through Thrum's editing efforts that Fornander's *Collection of Hawaiian Antiquities and Folklore* was first published.

While this anthology of tales represents the very best of the English versions of an Hawaiian view of the sacred and profane, the reader should be aware that the text has been filtered through the pen of outsiders who often embellished, altered or even censored original material. Though the gist of the tale may be authentic, sometimes certain beliefs and "earthy" or "bawdy" elements have been removed. In an effort to present the lore of ancient Hawai'i to a Victorian audience, it was often necessary to introduce into a story such Christian notions as monogamous marriage so as not to offend prudish sensibilities. One can only smile at the discomfort Westervelt may have felt when presenting an Hawaiian tale which in its original version was not confined by conservative or timid sexuality. Koko Head, for example, was originally called Kohelepelepe ("vagina labia minor") in reference to the time when Pele was attacked by Kamapua'a. To save Pele from being raped by the pig demigod, her older sister Kapo detached her vagina, using it as a decoy to divert Kamapua'a, and then hurled it to O'ahu, where it landed at the current site called Koko Head Crater. The missionary cartographers must have been tortured for days before finally renaming the crater Koko Head!

Recently there has been an effort to translate Hawaiian tales collected in the nineteenth century into English without imposing the moral attitudes of earlier foreign writers. *Stories and Legends of Oahu* by Samuel M. Kamakau includes several "trickster" narratives that reflect the more lively and hilarious earthiness of the old Hawaiian storytellers while Steven Goldsberry's *Maui the Demi God* is an unfiltered account of the trickster Maui.

Even with cultural biases or subtle distortions, the stories reprinted in this collection still perpetuate the beauty and mystery of Hawaiian sacred tradition. They serve as an excellent first introduction to the myths, legends and folk tales which once bonded people and the spirit realm in a cosmic unity of purpose. For those without the benefit of a learned *kapuna* to weave history and lore into a tapestry of cultural visions, the written word is a necessary first beginning. Hopefully, after reading this collection, the reader will take the next step and visit some of the sites mentioned in the text. Sitting quietly in the vicinity of a beach, stone, mountain or valley described in these tales, see if you don't experience the transforming power of the sacred narratives which for centuries have excited the souls of Polynesians. If even a small glimpse of that vision is afforded to you, then never again will you be able to see the lands and seas of Hawai'i in quite the same light. Those who are most fortunate will recognize the *mana* of an older sense of place which must be respected, perpetuated and wherever possible, restored.

HAWAIIAN FOLK TALES

I

LEGENDS RESEMBLING OLD TESTA-
MENT HISTORY

REV. C. M. HYDE, D. D.

IN the first volume of Judge Fornander's elaborate
work on "The Polynesian Race" he has given
some old Hawaiian legends which closely resemble
the Old Testament history. How shall we account
for such coincidences?

Take, for instance, the Hawaiian account of the
Creation. The *Kane, Ku,* and *Lono:* or, Sunlight, Substance, and Sound,—these constituted a triad named
Ku-Kaua-Kahi, or the Fundamental Supreme Unity.
In worship the reverence due was expressed by such
epithets as *Hi-ka-po-loa, Oi-e,* Most Excellent, etc.
"These gods existed from eternity, from and before
chaos, or, as the Hawaiian term expressed it, '*mai ka
po mai*' (from the time of night, darkness, chaos).
By an act of their will these gods dissipated or broke
into pieces the existing, surrounding, all-containing *po,*
night, or chaos. By this act light entered into space.
They then created the heavens, three in number, as a
place to dwell in; and the earth to be their footstool,
he keehina honua a Kane. Next they created the sun,

moon, stars, and a host of angels, or spirits — *i kini akua* — to minister to them. Last of all they created man as the model, or in the likeness of Kane. The body of the first man was made of red earth — *lepo ula*, or *alaea* — and the spittle of the gods — *wai nao*. His head was made of a whitish clay — *palolo* — which was brought from the four ends of the world by Lono. When the earth-image of Kane was ready, the three gods breathed into its nose, and called on it to rise, and it became a living being. Afterwards the first woman was created from one of the ribs — *lalo puhaka* — of the man while asleep, and these two were the progenitors of all mankind. They are called in the chants and in various legends by a large number of different names; but the most common for the man was Kumuhonua, and for the woman Keolakuhonua [or *Lalahonua*].

" Of the creation of animals these chants are silent; but from the pure tradition it may be inferred that the earth at the time of its creation or emergence from the watery chaos was stocked with vegetable and animal. The animals specially mentioned in the tradition as having been created by Kane were hogs (*puaa*), dogs (*ilio*), lizards or reptiles (*moo*).

" Another legend of the series, that of *Wela-ahi-lani*, states that after Kane had destroyed the world by fire, on account of the wickedness of the people then living, he organized it as it now is, and created the first man and the first woman, with the assistance of Ku and Lono, nearly in the same manner as narrated in the former legend of Kumuhonua. In this legend the man is called Wela-ahi-lani, and the woman is called Owe."

Of the primeval home, the original ancestral seat of mankind, Hawaiian traditions speak in highest praise. "It had a number of names of various meanings, though the most generally occurring, and said to be the oldest, was *Kalana-i-hau-ola* (Kalana with the life-giving dew). It was situated in a large country, or continent, variously called in the legends Kahiki-honua-kele, Kahiki-ku, Kapa-kapa-ua-a-Kane, Molo-lani. Among other names for the primary homestead, or paradise, are *Pali-uli* (the blue mountain), *Aina-i-ka-kaupo-o-Kane* (the land in the heart of Kane), *Aina-wai-akua-a-Kane* (the land of the divine water of Kane). The tradition says of Pali-uli, that it was a sacred, tabooed land; that a man must be righteous to attain it; if faulty or sinful he will not get there; if he looks behind he will not get there; if he prefers his family he will not enter Pali-uli." "Among other adornments of the Polynesian Paradise, the Kalana-i-hau-ola, there grew the *Ulu kapu a Kane*, the breadfruit tabooed for Kane, and the *ohia hemolele*, the sacred apple-tree. The priests of the olden time are said to have held that the tabooed fruits of these trees were in some manner connected with the trouble and death of Kumuhonua and Lala-honua, the first man and the first woman. Hence in the ancient chants he is called *Kane-laa-uli*, *Kumu-uli*, *Kulu-ipo*, the fallen chief, he who fell on account of the tree, or names of similar import."

According to those legends of Kumuhonua and

Wela-ahi-lani, "at the time when the gods created the stars, they also created a multitude of angels, or spirits (*i kini akua*), who were not created like men, but made from the spittle of the gods (*i kuhaia*), to be their servants or messengers. These spirits, or a number of them, disobeyed and revolted, because they were denied the *awa;* which means that they were not permitted to be worshipped, *awa* being a sacrificial offering and sign of worship. These evil spirits did not prevail, however, but were conquered by Kane, and thrust down into uttermost darkness (*ilalo loa i ka po*). The chief of these spirits was called by some Kanaloa, by others Milu, the ruler of Po; Akua ino; Kupu ino, the evil spirit. Other legends, however, state that the veritable and primordial lord of the Hawaiian inferno was called Manua. The inferno itself bore a number of names, such as Po-pau-ole, Po-kua-kini, Po-kini-kini, Po-papa-ia-owa, Po-ia-milu. Milu, according to those other legends, was a chief of superior wickedness on earth who was thrust down into Po, but who was really both inferior and posterior to Manua. This inferno, this Po, with many names, one of which remarkably enough was *Ke-po-lua-ahi*, the pit of fire, was not an entirely dark place. There was light of some kind and there was fire. The legends further tell us that when Kane, Ku, and Lono were creating the first man from the earth, Kanaloa was present, and in imitation of Kane, attempted to make another man out of the earth. When his clay model was ready, he called to it to become alive, but no life came to it. Then Kanaloa became very angry, and said to Kane,

'I will take your man, and he shall die,' and so it happened. Hence the first man got his other name *Kumu-uli*, which means a fallen chief, *he 'lii kahuli.* . . . With the Hawaiians, Kanaloa is the personified spirit of evil, the origin of death, the prince of Po, or chaos, and yet a revolted, disobedient spirit, who was conquered and punished by Kane. The introduction and worship of Kanaloa, as one of the great gods in the Hawaiian group, can be traced back only to the time of the immigration from the southern groups, some eight hundred years ago. In the more ancient chants he is never mentioned in conjunction with Kane, Ku, and Lono, and even in later Hawaiian mythology he never took precedence of Kane. The Hawaiian legend states that the oldest son of Kumuhonua, the first man, was called Laka, and that the next was called Ahu, and that Laka was a bad man; he killed his brother Ahu.

"There are these different Hawaiian genealogies, going back with more or less agreement among themselves to the first created man. The genealogy of Kumuhonua gives thirteen generations inclusive to Nuu, or Kahinalii, or the line of Laka, the oldest son of Kumuhonua. (The line of Seth from Adam to Noah counts ten generations.) The second genealogy, called that of Kumu-uli, was of greatest authority among the highest chiefs down to the latest times, and it was taboo to teach it to the common people. This genealogy counts fourteen generations from Huli-houna, the first man, to Nuu, or Nana-nuu, but inclusive, on the line of Laka. The third genealogy, which, properly speaking, is that of Paao, the high priest who came with Pili from Tahiti, about twenty-five generations ago, and was a reformer of the Hawaiian priesthood, and among whose descendants it has been preserved, counts only twelve generations from Kumuhonua to Nuu, on the line of Kapili, youngest son of Kumuhonua."

"In the Hawaiian group there are several legends of the Flood. One legend relates that in the time of Nuu, or Nana-nuu (also pronounced *lana*, that is, floating), the flood, *Kaiakahinalii*, came upon the earth, and destroyed all living beings; that Nuu, by command of his god, built a large vessel with a house on top of it, which was called and is referred to in chants as '*He waa halau Alii o ka Moku*,' the royal vessel, in which he and his family, consisting of his wife, Lilinoe, his three sons and their wives, were saved. When the flood subsided, Kane, Ku, and Lono entered the *waa halau* of Nuu, and told him to go out. He did so, and found himself on the top of Mauna Kea (the highest mountain on the island of Hawaii). He called a cave there after the name of his wife, and the cave remains there to this day — as the legend says in testimony of the fact. Other versions of the legend say that Nuu landed and dwelt in Kahiki-honua-kele, a large and extensive country." . . . . "Nuu left the vessel in the evening of the day and took with him a pig, cocoanuts, and *awa* as an offering to the god Kane. As he looked up he saw the moon in the sky. He thought it was the god, saying to himself, 'You are Kane, no doubt, though you have transformed yourself to my sight.' So he worshipped the moon, and offered his offerings. Then Kane descended on the rainbow and spoke reprovingly to Nuu, but on account of the mistake Nuu escaped punishment, having asked pardon of Kane." . . . "Nuu's three sons were Nalu-akea, Nalu-hoo-hua, and Nalu-mana-mana. In the tenth generation from Nuu arose Lua-nuu, or the second Nuu, known also in the legend as Kane-hoa-lani, Kupule, and other names. The legend adds that by command of his god he was the first to introduce circumcision to be practised among his descendants. He left his native home and moved a long way off until he reached a land called Honua-ilalo, 'the southern country.' Hence he got the name Lalo-kona, and his wife was called Honua-po-ilalo. He was the father of Ku-nawao by his slave-woman Ahu (O-ahu) and of Kalani-menehune by his wife, Mee-hewa. Another says that the god Kane ordered Lua-nuu to go up on a mountain and perform a sacrifice there. Lua-nuu looked among the mountains of Kahiki-ku, but none of them appeared suitable for the purpose. Then Lua-nuu inquired of God where he might find a proper place. God replied to him : 'Go travel to the eastward, and where you find a sharp-peaked hill projecting precipitously into the ocean, that is the hill for the sacrifice.' Then Lua-nuu and his son, Kupulu-pulu-a-Nuu, and his servant, Pili-lua-nuu, started off in their boat to the eastward. In remembrance of this event the Hawaiians called the back of Kualoa *Koolau;* Oahu (after one of Lua-nuu's names), *Kane-hoa-*

lani; and the smaller hills in front of it were named *Kupu-pulu* and *Pili-lua-nuu.* Lua-nuu is the tenth descendant from Nuu by both the oldest and the youngest of Nuu's sons. This oldest son is represented to have been the progenitor of the *Kanaka-maoli,* the people living on the mainland of Kane (*Aina kumupuaa a Kane*): the youngest was the progenitor of the white people (*ka poe keokeo maoli*). This Lua-nuu (like Abraham, the tenth from Noah, also like Abraham), through his grandson, Kini-lau-a-mano, became the ancestor of the twelve children of the latter, and the original founder of the Menehune people, from whom this legend makes the Polynesian family descend."

The Rev. Sheldon Dibble, in his history of the Sandwich Islands, published at Lahainaluna, in 1843, gives a tradition which very much resembles the history of Joseph. "Waikelenuiaiku was one of ten brethren who had one sister. They were all the children of one father, whose name was Waiku. Waikelenuiaiku was much beloved by his father, but his brethren hated him. On account of their hatred they carried him and cast him into a pit belonging to Holonaeole. The oldest brother had pity on him, and gave charge to Holonaeole to take good care of him. Waikelenuiaiku escaped and fled to a country over which reigned a king whose name was Kamohoalii. There he was thrown into a dark place, a pit under ground, in which many persons were confined for various crimes. Whilst confined in this dark place he told his companions to dream dreams and tell

them to him. The night following four of the pris-
oners had dreams. The first dreamed that he saw a
ripe *ohia* (native apple), and his spirit ate it; the second
dreamed that he saw a ripe banana, and his spirit ate
it; the third dreamed that he saw a hog, and his spirit
ate it; and the fourth dreamed that he saw *awa*,
pressed out the juice, and his spirit drank it. The
first three dreams, pertaining to food, Waikelenuiaiku
interpreted unfavorably, and told the dreamers they
must prepare to die. The fourth dream, pertaining
to drink, he interpreted to signify deliverance and life.
The first three dreamers were slain according to the
interpretation, and the fourth was delivered and saved.
Afterward this last dreamer told Kamohoalii, the
king of the land, how wonderful was the skill of Waikelenuiaiku in interpreting dreams, and the king sent
and delivered him from prison and made him a principal chief in his kingdom."

Judge Fornander alludes to this legend, giving the
name, however, *Aukelenui-a-Iku*, and adding to it
the account of the hero's journey to the place where
the water of life was kept (*ka-wai-ola-loa-a-Kane*), his
obtaining it and therewith resuscitating his brothers,
who had been killed by drowning some years before.
Another striking similarity is that furnished to Judge
Fornander in the legend of *Ke-alii-waha-nui*: "He
was king of the country called Honua-i-lalo. He
oppressed the Menehune people. Their god Kane
sent Kane-apua and Kaneloa, his elder brother, to
bring the people away, and take them to the land
which Kane had given them, and which was called

Ka aina momona a Kane, or *Ka one lauena a Kane*, and also *Ka aina i ka haupo a Kane*. The people were then told to observe the four Ku days in the beginning of the month as *Kapu-hoano* (sacred or holy days), in remembrance of this event, because they thus arose (*Ku*) to depart from that land. Their offerings on the occasion were swine and goats." The narrator of the legend explains that formerly there were goats without horns, called *malailua*, on the slopes of Mauna Loa on Hawaii, and that they were found there up to the time of Kamehameha I. The legend further relates that after leaving the land of Honualalo, the people came to the *Kai-ula-a-Kane* (the Red Sea of Kane); that they were pursued by Ke-alii-waha-nui; that Kane-apua and Kanaloa prayed to Lono, and finally reached the *Aina lauena a Kane*.

"In the famous Hawaiian legend of *Hiiaka-i-ka-poli-o-Pele*, it is said that when Hiiaka went to the island of Kauai to recover and restore to life the body of Lohiau, the lover of her sister, Pele, she arrived at the foot of the Kalalau Mountain shortly before sunset. Being told by her friends at Haena that there would not be daylight sufficient to climb the *pali* (precipice) and get the body out of the cave in which it was hidden, she prayed to her gods to keep the sun stationary (*i ka muli o Hea*) over the brook Hea, until she had accomplished her object. The prayer was heard, the mountain was climbed, the guardians of the cave vanquished, and the body recovered."

A story of retarding the sun and making the day

longer to accomplish his purpose is told of Maui-a-
kalana, according to Dibble's history.

Judge Fornander alludes to one other legend with
incidents similar to the Old Testament history wherein
"Na-ula-a-Maihea, an Oahu prophet, left Oahu for
Kauai, was upset in his canoe, was swallowed by a
whale, and thrown up alive on the beach at Wailua,
Kauai."

Judge Fornander says that, when he first heard the
legend of the two brother prophets delivering the
Menehune people, "he was inclined to doubt its
genuineness and to consider it as a paraphrase or adap-
tation of the Biblical account by some semi-civilized
or semi-Christianized Hawaiian, after the discovery of
the group by Captain Cook. But a larger and better
acquaintance with Hawaiian folk-lore has shown that
though the details of the legend, as interpreted by the
Christian Hawaiian from whom it was received, may
possibly in some degree, and unconsciously to him,
perhaps, have received a Biblical coloring, yet the main
facts of the legend, with the identical names of persons
and places, are referred to more or less distinctly in
other legends of undoubted antiquity." And the Rev.
Mr. Dibble, in his history, says of these Hawaiian
legends, that "they were told to the missionaries before
the Bible was translated into the Hawaiian tongue, and
before the people knew much of sacred history. The
native who acted as assistant in translating the history
of Joseph was forcibly struck with its similarity to their
ancient tradition. Neither is there the least room for
supposing that the songs referred to are recent inven-

tions. They can all be traced back for generations, and are known by various persons residing on different islands who have had no communication with each other. Some of them have their date in the reign of some ancient king, and others have existed time out of mind. It may also be added, that both their narrations and songs are known the best by the very oldest of the people, and those who never learned to read; whose education and training were under the ancient system of heathenism."

"Two hypotheses," says Judge Fornander, "may with some plausibility be suggested to account for this remarkable resemblance of folk-lore. One is, that during the time of the Spanish galleon trade, in the sixteenth and seventeenth centuries, between the Spanish Main and Manila, some shipwrecked people, Spaniards and Portuguese, had obtained sufficient influence to introduce these scraps of Bible history into the legendary lore of this people. . . . On this first hypothesis I remark that, if the shipwrecked foreigners were educated men, or only possessed of such Scriptural knowledge as was then imparted to the commonality of laymen, it is morally impossible to conceive that a Spaniard of the sixteenth century should confine his instruction to some of the leading events of the Old Testament, and be totally silent upon the Christian dispensation, and the cruciolatry, mariolatry, and hagiolatry of that day. And it is equally impossible to conceive that the Hawaiian listeners, chiefs, priests, or commoners, should have retained and incorporated so much of the former in their own folk-lore, and yet have utterly forgotten every item bearing upon the latter.

"The other hypothesis is, that at some remote period either a body of the scattered Israelites had arrived at these islands direct, or in Malaysia, before the exodus of 'the Polynesian family,' and thus imparted a knowledge of their doctrines, of the early life of their ancestors, and of some of their peculiar customs, and that having been absorbed by the people among whom they found a refuge, this is all that remains to attest their presence—intellectual tombstones over a lost and forgotten race, yet sufficient after twenty-six centuries of silence to solve in some measure the ethnic puzzle of the lost tribes of Israel.   In regard to this second hypothesis, it is certainly more plausible and cannot be so curtly disposed of as the Spanish theory. . . . So far from being copied one from the other, they are in fact independent and original versions of a once common legend, or series of legends, held alike by Cushite, Semite, Turanian, and Aryan, up to a certain time, when the divergencies of national life and other causes brought other subjects peculiar to each other prominently in the foreground; and that as these divergencies hardened into system and creed, that grand old heirloom of a common past became overlaid and colored by the peculiar social and religious atmosphere through which it has passed up to the surface of the present time.   But besides this general reason for refusing to adopt the Israelitish theory, that the Polynesian legends were introduced by fugitive or emigrant Hebrews from the subverted kingdoms of

Israel or Judah, there is the more special reason to be added that the organization and splendor of Solomon's empire, his temple, and his wisdom became proverbial among the nations of the East subsequent to his time; on all these, the Polynesian legends are absolutely silent."

In commenting on the legend of *Hiiaka-i-ka-poli-o-Pele*, Judge Fornander says: "If the Hebrew legend of Joshua or a Cushite version give rise to it, it only brings down the community of legends a little later in time. And so would the legend of *Naulu-a-Maihea*, . . . unless the legend of Jonah, with which it corresponds in a measure, as well as the previous legend of Joshua and the sun, were Hebrew anachronisms compiled and adapted in later times from long antecedent materials, of which the Polynesian references are but broken and distorted echoes, bits of legendary mosaics, displaced from their original surroundings and made to fit with later associations."

In regard to the account of the Creation, he remarks that "the Hebrew legend infers that the god Elohim existed contemporaneously with and apart from the chaos. The Hawaiian legend makes the three great gods, Kane, Ku, and Lono, evolve themselves out of chaos. . . . The order of creation, according to Hawaiian folk-lore, was that after Heaven and earth had been separated, and the ocean had been stocked with its animals, the stars were created, then the moon, then the sun." Alluding to the fact that the account in Genesis is truer to nature, Judge Fornander nevertheless propounds the inquiry whether this fact may not "indicate that the Hebrew text is a later emendation of an older but once common tradition"?

Highest antiquity is claimed for Hawaiian traditions in regard to events subsequent to the creation of man. "In one of the sacrificial hymns of the Marquesans, when human victims were offered, frequent allusions were made to 'the red apples eaten in Naoau,' . . . and to the 'tabooed apples of Atea,' as the cause of death, wars, pestilence, famine, and other calamities, only to be averted or atoned for by the sacrifice of human victims. The close connection between the Hawaiian and the Marquesan legends indicates a common origin, and that origin can be no other than that from which the Chaldean and Hebrew legends of sacred trees, disobedience, and fall also sprang." In comparison of "the Hawaiian myth of Kanaloa as a fallen angel antagonistic to the great gods, as the spirit of evil and death in the world, the Hebrew legends are more vague and indefinite as to the existence of an evil principle. The serpent of Genesis, the Satan of Job, the Hillel of Isaiah, the dragon of the Apocalypse — all point, however, to the same underlying idea that the first cause of sin, death, evil, and calamities, was to be found in disobedience and revolt from God. They appear as disconnected scenes of a once grand drama that in olden times riveted the attention of mankind, and of which, strange to say, the clearest synopsis and the most coherent recollection are, so far, to be found in Polynesian traditions. It is probably in vain to inquire with whom the legend of an evil spirit and his operations in Heaven and on earth had its origin. Notwithstanding the apparent unity of design and remarkable coincidence in many points, yet the differences in coloring, detail, and presentation are too great to suppose the legend borrowed by one from either of the others. It probably descended to the Chaldeans, Polynesians, and Hebrews alike, from a source or people anterior to themselves, of whom history now is silent."

II

EXPLOITS OF MAUI

REV. A. O. FORBES

I.—SNARING THE SUN

MAUI was the son of Hina-lau-ae and Hina, and they dwelt at a place called Makalia, above Kahakuloa, on West Maui. Now, his mother Hina made *kapas*. And as she spread them out to dry, the days were so short that she was put to great trouble and labor in hanging them out and taking them in day after day until they were dry. Maui, seeing this, was filled with pity for her, for the days were so short that, no sooner had she got her kapas all spread out to dry, than the Sun went down, and she had to take them in again. So he determined to make the Sun go slower. He first went to Wailohi, in Hamakua, on East Maui, to observe the motions of the Sun. There he saw that it rose toward Hana. He then went up on Haleakala, and saw that the Sun in its course came directly over that mountain. He then went home again, and after a few days went to a place called Paeloko, at Waihee. There he cut down all the cocoanut-trees, and gathered the fibre of the cocoanut husks in great quantity. This he manufactured into strong cord. One Moemoe, seeing this,

said tauntingly to him: "Thou wilt never catch the
Sun. Thou art an idle nobody."

Maui answered: "When I conquer my enemy, and
my desire is attained, I will be your death." So he
went up Haleakala again, taking his cord with him.
And when the Sun arose above where he was stationed, he prepared a noose of the cord and, casting
it, snared one of the Sun's larger beams and broke it
off. And thus he snared and broke off, one after
another, all the strong rays of the Sun.

Then shouted he exultingly: "Thou art my captive, and now I will kill thee for thy going so swiftly."

And the Sun said: "Let me live, and thou shalt see
me go more slowly hereafter. Behold, hast thou not
broken off all my strong legs, and left me only the
weak ones?"

So the agreement was made, and Maui permitted
the Sun to pursue its course, and from that time on it
went more slowly; and that is the reason why the
days are longer at one season of the year than at
another. It was this that gave the name to that
mountain, which should properly be called *Alehe-ka-la*
(sun snarer), and not *Haleakala*.

When Maui returned from this exploit, he went to
find Moemoe, who had reviled him. But that individ-
ual was not at home. He went on in his pursuit till
he came upon him at a place called Kawaiopilopilo,
on the shore to the eastward of the black rock called
Kekaa, north of Lahaina. Moemoe dodged him up
hill and down, until at last Maui, growing wroth,
leaped upon and slew the fugitive. And the dead

body was transformed into a long rock, which is there to this day, by the side of the road.

II.—THE ORIGIN OF FIRE

Maui and Hina dwelt together, and to them were born four sons, whose names were Maui-mua, Maui-hope, Maui-kiikii, and Maui-o-ka-lana. These four were fishermen. One morning, just as the edge of the Sun lifted itself up, Maui-mua roused his brethren to go fishing. So they launched their canoe from the beach at Kaupo, on the island of Maui, where they were dwelling, and proceeded to the fishing ground. Having arrived there, they were beginning to fish, when Maui-o-ka-lana saw the light of a fire on the shore they had left, and said to his brethren: "Behold, there is a fire burning. Whose can this fire be?"

And they answered: "Whose, indeed? Let us return to the shore, that we may get our food cooked; but first let us get some fish."

So, after they had obtained some fish, they turned toward the shore; and when the canoe touched the beach Maui-mua leaped ashore and ran toward the spot where the fire had been burning. Now, the curly-tailed *alae* (mud-hens) were the keepers of the fire; and when they saw him coming they scratched the fire out and flew away. Maui-mua was defeated, and returned to the house to his brethren.

Then said they to him: "How about the fire?"

"How, indeed?" he answered. "When I got there, behold, there was no fire; it was out. I supposed some man had the fire, and behold, it was not so; the alae are the proprietors of the fire, and our bananas are all stolen."

When they heard that, they were filled with anger, and decided not to go fishing again, but to wait for the next appearance of the fire. But after many days had passed without their seeing the fire, they went fishing again, and behold, there was the fire! And so they were continually tantalized. Only when they were out fishing would the fire appear, and when they returned they could not find it.

This was the way of it. The curly-tailed alae knew that Maui and Hina had only these four sons, and if any of them stayed on shore to watch the fire while the others were out in the canoe the alae knew it by counting those in the canoe, and would not light the fire. Only when they could count four men in the canoe would they light the fire. So Maui-mua thought it over, and said to his brethren: "To-morrow morning do you go fishing, and I will stay ashore. But do you take the calabash and dress it in kapa, and put it in my place in the canoe, and then go out to fish."

They did so, and when they went out to fish the next morning, the alae counted and saw four figures in the canoe, and then they lit the fire and put the bananas on to roast. Before they were fully baked one of the alae cried out: "Our dish is cooked! Behold, Hina has a smart son."

And with that, Maui-mua, who had stolen close to them unperceived, leaped forward, seized the curly-tailed alae and exclaimed: "Now I will kill you, you scamp of an alae! Behold, it is you who are keeping the fire from us. I will be the death of you for this."

Then answered the alae: "If you kill me the secret dies with me, and you won't get the fire." As Maui-mua began to wring its neck, the alae again spoke, and said: "Let me live, and you shall have the fire."

So Maui-mua said: "Tell me, where is the fire?"

The alae replied: "It is in the leaf of the a-pe plant" (*Alocasia macrorrhiza*).

So, by the direction of the alae, Maui-mua began to rub the leaf-stalk of the ape-plant with a piece of stick, but the fire would not come. Again he asked: "Where is this fire that you are hiding from me?"

The alae answered: "In a green stick."

And he rubbed a green stick, but got no fire. So it went on, until finally the alae told him he would find it in a dry stick; and so, indeed, he did. But Maui-mua, in revenge for the conduct of the alae, after he had got the fire from the dry stick, said: "Now, there is one thing more to try." And he rubbed the top of the alae's head till it was red with blood, and the red spot remains there to this day.

III

PELE AND THE DELUGE

REV. A. O. FORBES

ALL volcanic phenomena are associated in Hawaiian legendary lore with the goddess Pele; and it is a somewhat curious fact that to the same celebrated personage is also attributed a great flood that occurred in ancient times. The legends of this flood are various, but mainly connected with the doings of Pele in this part of the Pacific Ocean. The story runs thus:

Kahinalii was the mother of Pele; Kanehoalani was her father; and her two brothers were Kamohoalii and Kahuilaokalani. Pele was born in the land of Hapakuela, a far-distant land at the edge of the sky, toward the southwest. There she lived with her parents until she was grown up, when she married Wahialoa; and to these were born a daughter named Laka, and a son named Menehune. But after a time Pele's husband, Wahialoa, was enticed away from her by Pelekumulani. The deserted Pele, being much displeased and troubled in mind on account of her husband, started on her travels in search of him, and came in the direction of the Hawaiian Islands. Now, at that time these islands were a vast waste. There was no sea, nor was there any fresh water. When Pele set

36

out on her journey, her parents gave her the sea to go with her and bear her canoes onward. So she sailed forward, flood-borne by the sea, until she reached the land of Pakuela, and thence onward to the land of Kanaloa. From her head she poured forth the sea as she went, and her brothers composed the celebrated ancient mele:

> O the sea, the great sea!
> Forth bursts the sea:
> Behold, it bursts on Kanaloa!

But the waters of the sea continued to rise until only the highest points of the great mountains, Haleakala, Maunakea, and Maunaloa, were visible; all else was covered. Afterward the sea receded until it reached its present level. This event is called the *Kai a Kahinalii* (Sea of Kahinalii), because it was from Kahinalii, her mother, that Pele received the gift of the sea, and she herself only brought it to Hawaii.

And from that time to this, Pele and all her family forsook their former land of Hapakuela and have dwelt in Hawaii-nei, Pele coming first and the rest following at a later time.

On her first arrival at Hawaii-nei, Pele dwelt on the island of Kauai. From there she went to Kalaupapa,[1] on the island of Molokai, and dwelt in the crater of Kauhako at that place; thence she departed to Puulaina,[2] near Lahainaluna, where she dug out that crater. Afterward she moved still further to Haleakala,

---

[1] Now the Leper Settlement.
[2] The hill visible from the Lahaina anchorage to the north of Lahainaluna School, and near to it.

where she stayed until she hollowed out that great crater; and finally she settled at Kilauea, on the island of Hawaii, where she has remained ever since.

[1] It is not a little remarkable that the progress of Pele, as stated in this tradition, agrees with geological observation in locating the earliest volcanic action in this group, on the island of Kauai, and the latest, on the island of Hawaii.—*Translator*.

IV

PELE AND KAHAWALI

FROM ELLIS'S "TOUR OF HAWAII"

IN the reign of Kealiikukii, an ancient king of
Hawaii, Kahawali, chief of Puna, and one of his
favorite companions went one day to amuse themselves with the *holua* (sled), on the sloping side of a
hill, which is still called *ka holua ana o Kahawali*
(Kahawali's sliding-place). Vast numbers of the
people gathered at the bottom of the hill to witness
the game, and a company of musicians and dancers
repaired thither to add to the amusement of the
spectators. The performers began their dance, and
amidst the sound of drums and the songs of the
musicians the sledding of Kahawali and his companion
commenced. The hilarity of the occasion attracted
the attention of Pele, the goddess of the volcano,
who came down from Kilauea to witness the sport.
Standing on the summit of the hill in the form of a
woman, she challenged Kahawali to slide with her.
He accepted the offer, and they set off together down
the hill. Pele, less acquainted with the art of balanc-
ing herself on the narrow sled than her rival, was
beaten, and Kahawali was applauded by the spectators
as he returned up the side of the hill.

Before starting again, Pele asked him to give her his *papa holua*, but he, supposing from her appearance that she was no more than a native woman, said: "*Aole!* (no!) Are you my wife, that you should obtain my sled?" And, as if impatient at being delayed, he adjusted his *papa*, ran a few yards to take a spring, and then, with this momentum and all his strength he threw himself upon it and shot down the hill.

Pele, incensed at his answer, stamped her foot on the ground and an earthquake followed, which rent the hill in sunder. She called, and fire and liquid lava arose, and, assuming her supernatural form, with these irresistible ministers of vengeance, she followed down the hill. When Kahawali reached the bottom, he arose, and on looking behind saw Pele, accompanied by thunder and lightning, earthquake, and streams of burning lava, closely pursuing him. He took up his broad spear which he had stuck in the ground at the beginning of the game, and, accompanied by his friend, fled for his life. The musicians, dancers, and crowds of spectators were instantly overwhelmed by the fiery torrent, which, bearing on its foremost wave the enraged goddess, continued to pursue Kahawali and his companion. They ran till they came to an eminence called Puukea. Here Kahawali threw off his cloak of netted ki leaves and proceeded toward his house, which stood near the shore. He met his favorite pig and saluted it by touching noses, then ran to the house of his mother, who lived at Kukii, saluted her by touching noses, and said: "*Aloha ino oe, eia ibonei paha oe e make ai, ke ai mainei Pele.*" (Compassion great to you! Close here, perhaps, is your death ; Pele comes devouring.) Leaving her, he met his wife, Kanakawahine, and saluted her. The burning torrent approached, and she said: "Stay with me here, and let us die together." He said: "No; I go, I go." He then saluted his two children, Poupoulu and Kaohe, and said, "*Ke ue nei au ia olua.*" (I grieve for you two.) The lava rolled near, and he ran till a deep chasm arrested his progress. He laid down his spear and walked over on it in safety. His friend called out for his help; he held out his spear over the chasm; his companion took hold of it and he drew him securely over. By this time Pele was coming down the chasm with accelerated motion. He ran till he reached Kula. Here he met his sister, Koai, but had only time to say, "*Aloha oe!*" (Alas for you!) and then ran on to the shore. His younger brother had just landed from his fishing-canoe, and had hastened to his house to provide for the safety of his family, when Kahawali arrived. He and his friend leaped into the canoe, and with his broad spear paddled out to sea. Pele, perceiving his escape, ran to the shore and hurled after him, with prodigious force, great stones and fragments of rock, which fell thickly around but did not strike his canoe. When he had paddled a short distance from the shore the *kumukahi* (east wind) sprung up. He fixed his broad spear upright in the canoe, that it might answer the double purpose of mast and sail, and by its aid he soon reached the island of Maui, where they rested one night and then proceeded to Lanai. The day following they moved on to Molokai, thence to Oahu, the abode of Kolonohailaau, his father, and Kanewahinekeaho, his sister, to whom he related his disastrous perils, and with whom he took up his permanent abode.

V

HIKU AND KAWELU

J. S. EMERSON

NOT far from the summit of Hualalai, on the island of Hawaii, in the cave on the southern side of the ridge, lived Hina and her son, the *kupua*, or demigod, Hiku. All his life long as a child and a youth, Hiku had lived alone with his mother on this mountain summit, and had never once been permitted to descend to the plains below to see the abodes of men and to learn of their ways. From time to time, his quick ear had caught the sound of the distant *hula* drum and the voices of the gay merrymakers. Often had he wished to see the fair forms of those who danced and sang in those far-off cocoanut groves. But his mother, more experienced in the ways of the world, had never given her consent. Now, at length, he felt that he was a man, and as the sounds of mirth arose on his ears, again he asked his mother to let him go for himself and mingle with the people on the shore. His mother, seeing that his mind was made up to go, reluctantly gave her consent and warned him not to stay too long, but to return in good time. So, taking in his hand his faithful arrow, *Pua Ne*, which he always carried, he started off.

This arrow was a sort of talisman, possessed of marvellous powers, among which were the ability to answer his call and by its flight to direct his journey.

Thus he descended over the rough clinker lava and through the groves of koa that cover the southwestern flank of the mountain, until, nearing its base, he stood on a distant hill; and consulting his arrow, he shot it far into the air, watching its bird-like flight until it struck on a distant hill above Kailua.   To this hill he rapidly directed his steps, and, picking up his arrow in due time, he again shot it into the air.   The second flight landed the arrow near the coast of Holualoa, some six or eight miles south of Kailua.   It struck on a barren waste of *pahoehoe*, or lava rock, beside the water-hole of *Waikalai*, known also as the *Wai a Hiku* (Water of Hiku), where to this day all the people of that vicinity go to get their water for man and beast.

Here he quenched his thirst, and nearing the village of Holualoa, again shot the arrow, which, instinct with life, entered the courtyard of the *alii*, or chief, of Kona, and from among the women who were there singled out the fair princess Kawelu, and landed at her feet. Seeing the noble bearing of Hiku as he approached to claim his arrow, she stealthily hid it and challenged him to find it.   Then Hiku called to the arrow, "*Pua ne! Pua ne!*" and the arrow replied, "*Ne!*" thus revealing its hiding-place.

This exploit with the arrow and the remarkable grace and personal beauty of the young man quite won the heart of the princess, and she was soon possessed by a strong passion for him, and determined to make him her husband.

With her wily arts she detained him for several days at her home, and when at last he was about to start for the mountain, she shut him up in the house and thus detained him by force. But the words of his mother, warning him not to remain too long, came to his mind, and he determined to break away from his prison. So he climbed up to the roof, and removing a portion of the thatch, made his escape.

When his flight was discovered by Kawelu, the infatuated girl was distracted with grief. Refusing to be comforted, she tasted no food, and ere many days had passed was quite dead. Messengers were despatched who brought back the unhappy Hiku, author of all this sorrow. Bitterly he wept over the corpse of his beloved, but it was now too late; the spirit had departed to the nether world, ruled over by Milu. And now, stung by the reproaches of her kindred and friends for his desertion, and urged on by his real love for the fair one, he resolved to attempt the perilous descent into the nether world and, if possible, to bring her spirit back.

With the assistance of her friends, he collected from the mountain slope a great quantity of the *kowali*, or convolvulus vine. He also prepared a hollow cocoanut shell, splitting it into two closely fitting parts. Then anointing himself with a mixture of rancid cocoanut and kukui oil, which gave him a very strong corpse-like odor, he started with his companions in the well-loaded canoes for a point in the sea where the sky comes down to meet the water.

Arrived at the spot, he directed his comrades to lower him into the abyss called by the Hawaiians the *Lua o Milu*. Taking with him his cocoanut-shell and seating himself astride of the cross-stick of the swing, or kowali, he was quickly lowered down by the long rope of kowali vines held by his friends in the canoe above.

Soon he entered the great cavern where the shades of the departed were gathered together. As he came among them, their curiosity was aroused to learn who he was. And he heard many remarks, such as "Whew! what an odor this corpse emits!" "He must have been long dead." He had rather overdone the matter of the rancid oil. Even Milu himself, as he sat on the bank watching the crowd, was completely deceived by the stratagem, for otherwise he never would have permitted this bold descent of a living man into his gloomy abode.

The Hawaiian swing, it should be remarked, unlike ours, has but one rope supporting the cross-stick on which the person is seated. Hiku and his swing attracted considerable attention from the lookers-on. One shade in particular watched him most intently; it was his sweetheart, Kawelu. A mutual recognition took place, and with the permission of Milu she darted up to him and swung with him on the kowali. But even she had to avert her face on account of his corpse-like odor. As they were enjoying together this favorite Hawaiian pastime of *lele kowali*, by a preconcerted signal the friends above were informed of the success of his ruse and were now rapidly drawing them up.

At first she was too much absorbed in the sport to notice this. When at length her attention was aroused by seeing the great distance of those beneath her, like a butterfly she was about to flit away, when the crafty Hiku, who was ever on the alert, clapped the cocoanut-shells together, imprisoning her within them, and was then quickly drawn up to the canoes above.

With their precious burden, they returned to the shores of Holualoa, where Hiku landed and at once repaired to the house where still lay the body of his beloved. Kneeling by its side, he made a hole in the great toe of the left foot, into which with great difficulty he forced the reluctant spirit, and in spite of its desperate struggles he tied up the wound so that it could not escape from the cold, clammy flesh in which it was now imprisoned. Then he began to *lomilomi*, or rub and chafe the foot, working the spirit further and further up the limb.

Gradually, as the heart was reached, the blood began once more to flow through the body, the chest began gently to heave with the breath of life, and soon the spirit gazed out through the eyes. Kawelu was now restored to consciousness, and seeing her beloved Hiku bending tenderly over her, she opened her lips and said: "How could you be so cruel as to leave me?"

All remembrance of the Lua o Milu and of her meeting him there had disappeared, and she took up the thread of consciousness just where she had left it a few days before at death. Great joy filled the hearts of the people of Holualoa as they welcomed back to their midst the fair Kawelu and the hero, Hiku, from whom she was no more to be separated.

LOCATION OF THE LUA O MILU

In the myth of Hiku and Kawelu, the entrance to the Lua o Milu is placed out to sea opposite Holualoa and a few miles south of Kailua. But the more usual account of the natives is, that it was situated at the mouth of the great valley of Waipio, in a place called Keoni, where the sands have long since covered up and concealed from view this passage from the upper to the nether world.

Every year, so it is told, the procession of ghosts called by the natives *Oio*, marches in solemn state down the Mahiki road, and at this point enters the Lua o Milu. A man, recently living in Waimea, of the best reputation for veracity, stated that about thirty or more years ago, he actually saw this ghostly company. He was walking up this road in the evening, when he saw at a distance the *Oio* appear, and knowing that should they encounter him his death would be inevitable, he discreetly hid himself behind a tree and, trembling with fear, gazed in silence at the dread spectacle. There was Kamehameha, the conqueror, with all his chiefs and warriors in military array, thousands of heroes who had won renown in the olden time. Though all were silent as the grave, they kept perfect step as they marched along, and passing through the woods down to Waipio, disappeared from his view.

In connection with the foregoing, Professor W. D. Alexander kindly contributes the following:

"The valley of Waipio is a place frequently celebrated in the songs and traditions of Hawaii, as having been the abode of Akea and Milu, the first kings of the island. . . .

"Some said that the souls of the departed went to the *Po* (place of night), and were annihilated or eaten by the gods there. Others said that some went to the regions of Akea and Milu. Akea (Wakea), they said, was the first king of Hawaii. At the expiration of his reign, which terminated with his life at Waipio, where we then were, he descended to a region far below, called Kapapahanaumoku (the island bearing rock or stratum), and founded a kingdom there. Milu, who was his successor, and reigned in Hamakua, descended, when he died, to Akea and shared the government of the place with him. Their land is a place of darkness; their food lizards and butterflies. There are several streams of water, of which they drink, and some said that there were large kahilis and wide-spreading kou trees, beneath which they reclined."[1]

"They had some very indistinct notion of a future state of happiness and of misery. They said that, after death, the ghost went first to the region of Wakea, the name of their first reputed progenitor, and if it had observed the religious rites and ceremonies, was entertained and allowed to remain there. That was a place of houses, comforts, and pleasures.

[1] Ellis's "Polynesian Researches," pp. 365-7.

If the soul had failed to be religious, it found no one there to entertain it, and was forced to take a desperate leap into a place of misery below, called Milu.

"There were several precipices, from the verge of which the unhappy ghosts were supposed to take the leap into the region of woe; three in particular, one at the northern extremity of Hawaii, one at the western termination of Maui, and the third at the northern point of Oahu."[1]

Near the northwest point of Oahu is a rock called Leina Kauhane, where the souls of the dead descended into Hades.   In New Zealand the same term, "Reinga" (the leaping place), is applied to the North Cape.   The Marquesans have a similar belief in regard to the northermost island of their group, and apply the same term, "Reinga," to their Avernus.

[1] Dibble's History, p. 99.

VI

LONOPUHA; OR, ORIGIN OF THE ART OF HEALING IN HAWAII

TRANSLATED BY THOS. G. THRUM

DURING the time that Milu was residing at Waipio, Hawaii, the year of which is unknown, there came to these shores a number of people, with their wives, from that vague foreign land, Kahiki. But they were all of godly kind (*ano akua nae*), it is said, and drew attention as they journeyed from place to place. They arrived first at Niihau, and from there they travelled through all the islands. At Hawaii they landed at the south side, thence to Puna, Hilo, and settled at Kukuihaele, Hamakua, just above Waipio.

On every island they visited there appeared various diseases, and many deaths resulted, so that it was said this was their doings, among the chiefs and people. The diseases that followed in their train were chills, fevers, headache, *pani*, and so on.

These are the names of some of these people: Kaalaenuiahina, Kahuilaokalani, Kaneikaulanaula, besides others. They brought death, but one Kamakanuiahailono followed after them with healing powers. This was perhaps the origin of sickness and the art of healing with medicines in Hawaii.

As has been said, diseases settled on the different islands like an epidemic, and the practice of medicine ensued, for Kamakanuiahailono followed them in their journeyings. He arrived at Kau, stopping at Kiolakaa, on the west side of Waiohinu, where a great multitude of people were residing, and Lono was their chief. The stranger sat on a certain hill, where many of the people visited him, for the reason that he was a new-comer, a custom that is continued to this day. While there he noticed the redness of skin of a certain one of them, and remarked, "Oh, the redness of skin of that man!"

The people replied, "Oh, that is Lono, the chief of this land, and he is a farmer."

He again spoke, asserting that his sickness was very great; for through the redness of the skin he knew him to be a sick man.

They again replied that he was a healthy man, "but you consider him very sick." He then left the residents and set out on his journey.

Some of those who heard his remarks ran and told the chief the strange words, "that he was a very sick man." On hearing this, Lono raised up his *oo* (digger) and said, "Here I am, without any sign of disease, and yet I am sick." And as he brought down his *oo* with considerable force, it struck his foot and pierced it through, causing the blood to flow freely, so that he fell and fainted away. At this, one of the men seized a pig and ran after the stranger, who, hearing the pig squealing, looked behind him and saw the man running with it; and as he neared him he dropped it

before him, and told him of Lono's misfortune. Kamakanuiahailono then returned, gathering on the way the
young popolo seeds and its tender leaves in his garment
(*kihei*).   When he arrived at the place where the
wounded man was lying he asked for some salt, which
he took and pounded together with the popolo and
placed it with a cocoanut covering on the wound.
From then till night the flowing of the blood ceased.
After two or three weeks had elapsed he again took
his departure.

While he was leisurely journeying, some one breathing heavily approached him in the rear, and, turning
around, there was the chief, and he asked him : "What
is it, Lono, and where are you going?"

Lono replied, "You healed me; therefore, as soon
as you had departed I immediately consulted with my
successors, and have resigned my offices to them, so
that they will have control over all.   As for myself,
I followed after you, that you might teach me the art
of healing."

The *kahuna lapaau* (medical priest) then said, "Open
your mouth."   When Lono opened his mouth, the
kahuna spat into it,[1] by which he would become proficient in the calling he had chosen, and in which he
eventually became, in fact, very skilful.

As they travelled, he instructed Lono (on account
of the accident to his foot he was called Lonopuha) in
the various diseases, and the different medicines for the
proper treatment of each.   They journeyed through
Kau, Puna, and Hilo, thence onward to Hamakua as

[1] An initiatory act, as in the priesthood.

far as Kukuihaele. Prior to their arrival there, Kamakanuiahailono said to Lonopuha, "It is better that we
reside apart, lest your healing practice do not succeed;
but you settle elsewhere, so as to gain recognition from
your own skill."

For this reason, Lonopuha went on farther and
located in Waimanu, and there practised the art of
healing. On account of his labors here, he became
famous as a skilful healer, which fame Kamakanuiahailono and others heard of at Kukuihaele; but he
never revealed to *Kaalaenuiahina ma* (company) of his
teaching of Lonopuha, through which he became celebrated. It so happened that *Kaalaenuiahina ma* were
seeking an occasion to cause Milu's death, and he was
becoming sickly through their evil efforts.

When Milu heard of the fame of Lonopuha as a
skilful healer, because of those who were afflicted with
disease and would have died but for his treatment, he
sent his messenger after him. On arriving at Milu's
house, Lonopuha examined and felt of him, and then
said, "You will have no sickness, provided you be
obedient to my teachings." He then exercised his
art, and under his medical treatment Milu recovered.

Lonopuha then said to him: "I have treated you,
and you are well of the internal ailments you suffered
under, and only that from without remains. Now, you
must build a house of leaves and dwell therein in
quietness for a few weeks, to recuperate." These
houses are called *pipipi*, such being the place to which
invalids are moved for convalescent treatment unless
something unforeseen should occur.

Upon Milu's removal thereto, Lonopuha advised him as follows : " O King! you are to dwell in this house according to the length of time directed, in perfect quietness; and should the excitement of sports with attendant loud cheering prevail here, I warn you against these as omens of evil for your death; and I advise you not to loosen the *ti* leaves of your house to peep out to see the cause, for on the very day you do so, that day you will perish."

Some two weeks had scarcely passed since the King had been confined in accordance with the kahuna's instructions, when noises from various directions in proximity to the King's dwelling were heard, but he regarded the advice of the priest all that day. The cause of the commotion was the appearance of two birds playing in the air, which so excited the people that they kept cheering them all that day.

Three weeks had almost passed when loud cheering was again heard in Waipio, caused by a large bird decorated with very beautiful feathers, which flew out from the clouds and soared proudly over the *palis* (precipices) of Koaekea and Kaholokuaiwa, and poised gracefully over the people; therefore, they cheered as they pursued it here and there. Milu was much worried thereby, and became so impatient that he could no longer regard the priest's caution; so he lifted some of the ti leaves of his house to look out at the bird, when instantly it made a thrust at him, striking him under the armpit, whereby his life was taken and he was dead (*lilo ai kona ola a make iho la*).

The priest saw the bird flying with the liver of Milu;

therefore, he followed after it. When it saw that it was pursued, it immediately entered into a sunken rock just above the base of the precipice of Koaekea. As he reached the place, the blood was spattered around where the bird had entered. Taking a piece of garment (*pahoola*), he soaked it with the blood and returned and placed it in the opening in the body of the dead King and poured healing medicine on the wound, whereby Milu recovered. And the place where the bird entered with Milu's liver has ever since been called Keakeomilu (the liver of Milu).

A long while afterward, when this death of the King was as nothing (*i mea ole*), and he recovered as formerly, the priest refrained not from warning him, saying: "You have escaped from this death; there remains for you one other."

After Milu became convalescent from his recent serious experience, a few months perhaps had elapsed, when the surf at Waipio became very high and was breaking heavily on the beach. This naturally caused much commotion and excitement among the people, as the numerous surf-riders, participating in the sport, would land upon the beach on their surf-boards. Continuous cheering prevailed, and the hilarity rendered Milu so impatient at the restraint put upon him by the priest that he forsook his wise counsel and joined in the exhilarating sport.

Seizing a surf-board he swam out some distance to the selected spot for suitable surfs. Here he let the first and second combers pass him; but watching his opportunity he started with the momentum of the heavier third comber, catching the crest just right. Quartering on the rear of his board, he rode in with majestic swiftness, and landed nicely on the beach amid the cheers and shouts of the people. He then repeated the venture and was riding in as successfully, when, in a moment of careless abandon, at the place where the surfs finish as they break on the beach, he was thrust under and suddenly disappeared, while the surf-board flew from under and was thrown violently upon the shore. The people in amazement beheld the event, and wildly exclaimed: "Alas! Milu is dead! Milu is dead!" With sad wonderment they searched and watched in vain for his body. Thus was seen the result of repeated disobedience.

VII

A VISIT TO THE SPIRIT LAND; OR, THE STRANGE EXPERIENCE OF A WOMAN IN KONA, HAWAII

MRS. E. N. HALEY

KALIMA had been sick for many weeks, and at last died. Her friends gathered around her with loud cries of grief, and with many expressions of affection and sorrow at their loss they prepared her body for its burial.

The grave was dug, and when everything was ready for the last rites and sad act, husband and friends came to take a final look at the rigid form and ashen face before it was laid away forever in the ground. The old mother sat on the mat-covered ground beside her child, brushing away the intrusive flies with a piece of cocoanut-leaf, and wiping away the tears that slowly rolled down her cheeks. Now and then she would break into a low, heart-rending wail, and tell in a sob-choked, broken voice, how good this her child had always been to her, how her husband loved her, and how her children would never have any one to take her place. "Oh, why," she cried, "did the gods leave me? I am old and heavy with years; my back is bent and my eyes are getting dark. I cannot work, and am too old and weak to enjoy fishing in the sea, or dancing and feasting under the trees. But this my child loved all these things, and was so happy. Why is she taken and I, so useless, left?" And again that mournful, sob-choked wail broke on the still air, and was borne out to the friends gathered under the trees before the door, and was taken up and repeated until the hardest heart would have softened and melted at the sound. As they sat around on the mats looking at their dead and listening to the old mother, suddenly Kalima moved, took a long breath, and opened her eyes. They were frightened at the miracle, but so happy to have her back again among them.

The old mother raised her hands and eyes to heaven and, with rapt faith on her brown, wrinkled face, exclaimed: "The gods have let her come back! How they must love her!"

Mother, husband, and friends gathered around and rubbed her hands and feet, and did what they could for her comfort. In a few minutes she revived enough to say, "I have something strange to tell you."

Several days passed before she was strong enough to say more; then calling her relatives and friends about her, she told them the following weird and strange story:

"I died, as you know. I seemed to leave my body and stand beside it, looking down on what *was* me. The me that was standing there looked like the form I was looking at, only, I was alive and the other was dead. I gazed at my body for a few minutes, then turned and walked away. I left the house and village,

and walked on and on to the next village, and there I
found crowds of people,—Oh, so many people! The
place which I knew as a small village of a few houses
was a very large place, with hundreds of houses and
thousands of men, women, and children. Some of
them I knew and they spoke to me,—although that
seemed strange, for I knew they were dead,—but
nearly all were strangers. They were all so happy!
They seemed not to have a care; nothing to trouble
them. Joy was in every face, and happy laughter
and bright, loving words were on every tongue.

"I left that village and walked on to the next. I
was not tired, for it seemed no trouble to walk. It
was the same there; thousands of people, and every
one so joyous and happy. Some of these I knew.
I spoke to a few people, then went on again. I
seemed to be on my way to the volcano,—to Pele's
pit,—and could not stop, much as I wanted to do so.

"All along the road were houses and people, where
I had never known any one to live. Every bit
of good ground had many houses, and many, many
happy people on it. I felt so full of joy, too, that
my heart sang within me, and I was glad to be
dead.

"In time I came to South Point, and there, too,
was a great crowd of people. The barren point was a
great village. I was greeted with happy *alohas*, then
passed on. All through Kau it was the same, and I
felt happier every minute. At last I reached the volcano. There were some people there, but not so
many as at other places. They, too, were happy like

the others, but they said, 'You must go back to your body. You are not to die yet.'

"I did not want to go back. I begged and prayed to be allowed to stay with them, but they said, 'No, you must go back; and if you do not go willingly, we will make you go.'

"I cried and tried to stay, but they drove me back, even beating me when I stopped and would not go on. So I was driven over the road I had come, back through all those happy people. They were still joyous and happy, but when they saw that I was not allowed to stay, they turned on me and helped drive me, too.

"Over the sixty miles I went, weeping, followed by those cruel people, till I reached my home and stood by my body again. I looked at it and hated it. Was that my body? What a horrid, loathsome thing it was to me now, since I had seen so many beautiful, happy creatures! Must I go and live in that thing again? No, I would not go into it; I rebelled and cried for mercy.

"'You must go into it; we will make you!' said my tormentors. They took me and pushed me head foremost into the big toe.

"I struggled and fought, but could not help myself. They pushed and beat me again, when I tried for the last time to escape. When I passed the waist, I seemed to know it was of no use to struggle any more, so went the rest of the way myself. Then my body came to life again, and I opened my eyes.

"But I wish I could have stayed with those happy

people. It was cruel to make me come back. My other body was so beautiful, and I was so happy, so happy!"

VIII

KAPEEPEEKAUILA; OR, THE ROCKS OF KANA

REV. A. O. FORBES

ON the northern side of the island of Molokai, commencing at the eastern end and stretching along a distance of about twenty miles, the coast is a sheer precipice of black rock varying in height from eight hundred to two thousand feet. The only interruptions to the continuity of this vast sea wall are formed by the four romantic valleys of Pelekunu, Puaahaunui, Wailau, and Waikolu. Between the valleys of Pelekunu and Waikolu, juts out the bold, sharp headland of Haupu, forming the dividing ridge between them, and reminding one somewhat of an axe-head turned edge upward. Directly in a line with this headland, thirty or forty rods out in the ocean, arise abruptly from the deep blue waters the rocks of Haupu, three or four sharp, needle-like points of rock varying from twenty to one hundred feet in height. This is the spot associated with the legend of Kapeepeekauila, and these rocks stand like grim sentinels on duty at the eastern limit of what is now known as the settlement of Kalawao. The legend runs as follows:

Keahole was the father, Hiiaka-noholae was the

63

mother, and Kapeepeekauila was the son. This Kapeepeekauila was a hairy man, and dwelt on the ridge of Haupu.

Once on a time Hakalanileo and his wife Hina, the mother of Kana, came and dwelt in the valley of Pelekunu, on the eastern side of the ridge of Haupu.

Kapeepeekauila, hearing of the arrival of Hina, the beautiful daughter of Kalahiki, sent his children to fetch her. They went and said to Hina, "Our royal father desires you as his wife, and we have come for you."

"Desires me for what?" said she.

"Desires you for a wife," said they.

This announcement pleased the beautiful daughter of Kalahiki, and she replied, "Return to your royal father and tell him he shall be the husband and I will be the wife."

When this message was delivered to Kapeepeekauila, he immediately sent a messenger to the other side of the island to summon all the people from Keonekuina to Kalamaula; for we have already seen that he was a hairy man, and it was necessary that this blemish should be removed. Accordingly, when the people had all arrived, Kapeepeekauila laid himself down and they fell to work until the hairs were all plucked out. He then took Hina to wife, and they two dwelt together on the top of Haupu.

Poor Hakalanileo, the husband of Hina, mourned the loss of his companion of the long nights of winter and the shower-sprinkled nights of summer. Neither could he regain possession of her, for the ridge of

Haupu grew till it reached the heavens. He mourned and rolled himself in the dust in agony, and crossed his hands behind his back. He went from place to place in search of some powerful person who should be able to restore to him his wife. In his wanderings, the first person to whom he applied was Kamalala-walu, celebrated for strength and courage. This man, seeing his doleful plight, asked, "Why these tears, O my father?"

Hakalanileo replied, "Thy mother is lost."

"Lost to whom?"

"Lost to Kapeepee."

"What Kapeepee?"

"Kapeepee-kauila."

"What Kauila?"

"Kauila, the dauntless, of Haupu."

"Then, O father, thou wilt not recover thy wife. Our stick may strike; it will but hit the dust at his feet. His stick, when it strikes back, will hit the head. Behold, measureless is the height of Haupu."

Now, this Kamalalawalu was celebrated for his strength in throwing stones. Of himself, one side was stone, and the other flesh. As a test he seized a large stone and threw it upwards. It rose till it hit the sky and then fell back to earth again. As it came down, he turned his stony side toward it, and the collision made his side rattle. Hakalanileo looked on and sadly said, "Not strong enough."

On he went, beating his breast in his grief, till he came to the celebrated Niuloihiki. Question and answer passed between them, as in the former case, but

Niuloihiki replied, "It is hopeless; behold, measureless is the height of Haupu."

Again he prosecuted his search till he met the third man of fame, whose name was Kaulu. Question and answer passed, as before, and Kaulu, to show his strength, seized a river and held it fast in its course. But Hakalanileo mournfully said, "Not strong enough."

Pursuing his way with streaming eyes, he came to the fourth hero, Lonokaeho by name. As in the former cases, so in this, he received no satisfaction. These four were all he knew of who were foremost in prowess, and all four had failed him. It was the end, and he turned sadly toward the mountain forest, to return to his home.

Meantime, the rumor had reached the ears of Niheu, surnamed "the Rogue." Some one told him a father had passed along searching for some one able to recover him his wife.

"Where is this father of mine?" inquired Niheu.

"He has gone inland," was the reply.

"I 'll overtake him; he won't escape me," said Niheu. So he went after the old man, kicking over the trees that came in his way. The old man had gone on till he was tired and faint, when Niheu overtook him and brought him back to his house. Then Niheu asked him, "What made you go on without coming to the house of Niheu?"

"What, indeed," answered the old man; "as though I were not seeking to recover thy mother, who is lost!"

Then came question and answer, as in former cases, and Niheu said, "I fear thou wilt not recover thy wife, O my father. But let us go inland to the foster son of Uli." So they went. But Niheu ran on ahead and told Kana, the foster son of Uli: "Behold, here comes Hakalanileo, bereft of his wife. We are all beat."

"Where is he?" inquired Kana.

"Here he is, just arrived."

Kana looked forth, and Hakalanileo recoiled with fear at the blazing of his eyes.

Then spoke Niheu: "Why could you not wait before looking at our father? Behold, you have frightened him, and he has run back."

On this, Kana, remaining yet in the house, stretched forth his hand, and, grasping the old man in the distance, brought him back and sat him on his lap. Then Kana wept. And the impudent Niheu said, "Now you are crying; look out for the old man, or he will get water-soaked."

But Kana ordered Niheu to bestir himself and light a fire, for the tears of Kana were as the big dropping rains of winter, soaking the plain. And Kana said to the old man, "Now, dry yourself by the fire, and when you are warm, tell your story."

The old man obeyed, and when he was warm enough, told the story of his grief. Then said Kana, "Almost spent are my years; I am only waiting for death, and behold I have at last found a foeman worthy of my prowess."

Kana immediately espoused the cause of Hakalanileo, and ordered his younger brother, Niheu, to construct a canoe for the voyage. Poor Niheu worked and toiled without success until, in despair, he exclaimed, upbraidingly, "Thy work is not work; it is slavery. There thou dwellest at thy ease in thy retreat, while with thy foot thou destroyest my canoe."

Upon this, Kana pointed out to Niheu a bush, and said, "Can you pull up that bush?"

"Yes," replied Niheu, for it was but a small bush, and he doubted not his ability to root it up; so he pulled and tugged away, but could not loosen it.

Kana looking on, said, tauntingly, "Your foeman will not be overcome by you."

Then Kana stretched forth his hands, scratching among the forests, and soon had a canoe in one hand; a little more and another canoe appeared in the other hand. The twin canoes were named *Kaumueli*. He lifted them down to the shore, provided them with paddles, and then appointed fourteen rowers. Kana embarked with his magic rod called *Waka-i-lani*. Thus they set forth to wage war upon Kapeepeekauila. They went on until the canoes grounded on a hard ledge.

Niheu called out, "Behold, thou sleepest, O Kana, while we all perish."

Kana replied, "What is there to destroy us? Are not these the reefs of Haupu? Away with the ledges, the rock points, and the yawning chasms! Smite with *Waka-i-lani*, thy rod."

Niheu smote, the rocks crumbled to pieces, and the canoes were freed. They pursued their course again until Niheu, being on the watch, cried out, "Why sleepest thou, O Kana? Here we perish, again. Thy like for sleeping I never saw!"

"Wherefore perish?" said Kana.

"Behold," replied Niheu, "the fearful wall of water. If we attempt to pass it, it will topple over and destroy us all."

Then said Kana: "Behold, behind us the reefs of Haupu. That is the destruction passed. As for the destruction before us, smite with thy rod."

Niheu smote, the wall of water divided, and the canoes passed safely through. Then they went on their course again, as before. After a time, Niheu again called out, "Alas, again we perish. Here comes a great monster. If he falls upon us, we are all dead men."

And Kana said, "Look sharp, now, and when the pointed snout crosses our bow, smite with thy rod."

And he did so, and behold, this great thing was a monster fish, and when brought on board it became food for them all. So wonderfully great was this fish that its weight brought the rim of the canoes down to the water's edge.

They continued on their way, and next saw the open mouth of the sharp-toothed shark — another of the outer defences of Haupu—awaiting them.

"Smite with thy rod," ordered Kana.

Niheu smote, and the shark died.

Next they came upon the great turtle, another defence of Haupu. Again the sleepy Kana is aroused by the cry of the watchful Niheu, and the turtle is

slain by the stroke of the magic rod. All this was
during the night. At last, just as the edge of the
morning lifted itself from the deep, their mast became
entangled in the branches of the trees. Niheu flung
upward a stone. It struck. The branches came rat-
tling down, and the mast was free. On they went till
the canoes gently stood still. On this, Niheu cried
out, "Here you are, asleep again, O Kana, and the
canoes are aground!"

Kana felt beneath; there was no ground. He felt
above; the mast was entangled in weeds. He pulled,
and the weeds and earth came down together. The
smell of the fresh-torn weeds was wafted up to Hale-
huki, the house where Kapeepeekauila lived. His
people, on the top of Haupu, looked down on the
canoes floating at the foot. "Wondrous is the size
of the canoes!" they cried. "Ah! it is a load of *opihis*
(shell-fish) from Hawaii for Hina," for that was a
favorite dish with her.

Meantime, Kana despatched Niheu after his mother.
"Go in friendly fashion," said the former.

Niheu leaped ashore, but slipped and fell on the
smooth rocks. Back he went to the canoes.

"What sort of a coming back is this?" demanded
Kana.

"I slipped and fell, and just escaped with my life,"
answered Niheu.

"Back with you!" thundered Kana.

Again the luckless Niheu sprang ashore, but the
long-eyed sand-crabs (*ohiki-makaloa*) made the sand fly
with their scratching till his eyes were filled. Back to

the canoes again he went. "Got it all in my eyes!" said he, and he washed them out with sea-water.

"You fool!" shouted Kana; "what were you looking down for? The sand-crabs are not birds. If you had been looking up, as you ought, you would not have got the sand in your eyes. Go again!"

This time he succeeded, and climbed to the top of Haupu. Arriving at the house, Hale-huki, where Hina dwelt, he entered at once. Being asked "Why enterest thou this forbidden door?" he replied:

"Because I saw thee entering by this door. Hadst thou entered some other way, I should not have come in at the door." And behold, Kapeepeekauila and Hina sat before him. Then Niheu seized the hand of Hina and said, "Let us two go." And she arose and went.

When they had gone about half-way to the brink of the precipice, Kapeepeekauila exclaimed, "What is this? Is the woman gone?"

Mo-i, the sister of Kana, answered and said, "If you wish the woman, now is the time; you and I fight."

Great was the love of Kapeepeekauila for Hina, and he said, "No war dare touch Haupu; behold, it is a hill, growing even to the heavens." And he sent the *kolea* (plover) squad to desecrate the sacred locks of Niheu; for the locks of Niheu were *kapu*, and if they should be touched, he would relinquish Hina for very shame. So the kolea company sailed along in the air till they brushed against the sacred locks of Niheu, and for very shame he let go his mother and struck at the koleas with his rod and hit their tail feathers and knocked them all out, so that they remain tailless to this day. And he returned to the edge of the shore, while the koleas bore off Hina in triumph.

When Niheu reached the shore, he beat his forehead with stones till the blood flowed; a trick which Kana perceived from on board the canoes. And when Niheu went on board he said, "See! we fought and I got my head hurt."

But Kana replied, "There was no fight; you did it yourself, out of shame at your defeat."

And Niheu replied, "What, then, shall we fight?"

"Yes," said Kana, and he stood up.

Now, one of his legs was named Keauea and the other Kaipanea, and as he stood upon the canoes, he began to lengthen himself upward until the dwellers on top of Haupu exclaimed in terror, "We are all dead men! Behold, here is a great giant towering above us."

And Kapeepeekauila, seeing this, hastened to prune the branches of the kamani tree (*Calophyllum inophyllum*), so that the bluff should grow upward. And the bluff rose, and Kana grew. Thus they strove, the bluff rising higher and Kana growing taller, until he became as the stalk of a banana leaf, and gradually spun himself out till he was no thicker than a strand of a spider's web, and at last he yielded the victory to Kapeepeekauila.

Niheu, seeing the defeat of Kana, called out, "Lay yourself along to Kona, on Hawaii, to your grandmother, Uli."

And he laid himself along with his body in Kona, while his feet rested on Molokai. His grandmother in Kona fed him until he became plump and fat again.

Meanwhile, poor Niheu, watching at his feet on Molokai, saw their sides fill out with flesh while he was almost starved with hunger. "So, then," quoth he, "you are eating and growing fat while I die with hunger." And he cut off one of Kana's feet for revenge.

The sensation crept along up to his body, which lay in Kona, and Kana said to his grandmother, Uli, "I seem to feel a numbness creeping over me."

And she answered, and said, "Thy younger brother is hungry with watching, and seeing thy feet grow plump, he has cut off one of them; therefore this numbness."

Kana, having at last grown strong and fat, prepared to wage war again upon Kapeepeekauila. Food was collected in abundance from Waipio, and when it was prepared, they embarked again in their canoes and came back to Haupu, on Molokai. But his grandmother, Uli, had previously instructed him to first destroy all the branches of the kamani tree of Haupu. Then he showed himself, and began again to stretch upward and tower above the bluff. Kapeepeekauila hastened again to trim the branches of the kamani, that the bluff might grow as before; but behold, they were all gone! It was the end; Kapeepeekauila was at last vanquished. The victorious Kana recovered his sister, Mo-i, restored to poor Hakalanileo his wife, Hina, and then, tearing down the bluff of Haupu, kicked off large portions of it into the sea, where they stand to this day, and are called "The Rocks of Kana."

IX

KALELEALUAKA

DR. N. B. EMERSON

PART I

KAOPELE was born in Waipio, Hawaii. When born he did not breathe, and his parents were greatly troubled; but they washed his body clean, and having arrayed it in good clothes, they watched anxiously over the body for several days, and then, concluding it to be dead, placed it in a small cave in the face of the cliff. There the body remained from the summer month of *Ikiki* (July or August) to the winter month of *Ikua* (December or January), a period of six months.

At this time they were startled by a violent storm of thunder and lightning, and the rumbling of an earthquake. At the same time appeared the marvellous phenomenon of eight rainbows arching over the mouth of the cave. Above the din of the storm the parents heard the voice of the awakened child calling to them:

> " Let your love rest upon me,
> O my parents, who have thrust me forth,
> Who have left me in the cavernous cliff,
> Who have heartlessly placed me in the
> Cliff frequented by the tropic bird!

74

O Waiaalaia, my mother!
O Waimanu, my father!
Come and take me!''

The yearning love of the mother earnestly besought the father to go in quest of the infant; but he protested that search was useless, as the child was long since dead. But, unable longer to endure a woman's teasing, which is the same in all ages, he finally set forth in high dudgeon, vowing that in case of failure he would punish her on his return.

On reaching the place where the babe had been deposited, its body was not to be found. But lifting up his eyes and looking about, he espied the child perched on a tree, braiding a wreath from the scarlet flowers of the lehua (*Metrosideros polymorpha*). "I have come to take you home with me," said the father. But the infant made no answer. The mother received the child to her arms with demonstrations of the liveliest affection. At her suggestion they named the boy Kaopele, from the name of their goddess, Pele.

Six months after this, on the first day (*Hilo*) of the new moon, in the month of Ikiki, they returned home from working in the fields and found the child lying without breath, apparently dead. After venting their grief for their darling in loud lamentations, they erected a frame to receive its dead body.

Time healed the wounds of their affection, and after the lapse of six moons they had ceased to mourn, when suddenly they were affrighted by a storm of thunder and lightning, with a quaking of the earth, in the midst of which they distinguished the cry of their child, "Oh, come; come and take me!"

They, overjoyed at this second restoration of their child to them, and deeming it to be a miracle worked by their goddess, made up their minds that if it again fell into a trance they would not be anxious, since their goddess would awake their child and bring it to life again.

But afterward the child informed them of their mistake, saying: "This marvel that you see in me is a trance; when I pass into my deep sleep my spirit at once floats away in the upper air with the goddess, Poliahu. We are a numerous band of spirits, but I excel them in the distance of my flights. In one day I can compass this island of Hawaii, as well as Maui, Oahu, and Kauai, and return again. In my flights I have seen that Kauai is the richest of all the islands, for it is well supplied with food and fish, and it is abundantly watered. I intend to remain with you until I am grown; then I shall journey to Kauai and there spend the rest of my life." Thus Kaopele lived with his parents until he was grown, but his habit of trance still clung to him.

Then one day he filled them with grief by saying: "I am going, aloha."

They sealed their love for each other with tears and kisses, and he slept and was gone. He alighted at Kula, on Maui. There he engaged in cultivating food. When his crops were nearly ripe and ready to be eaten he again fell into his customary deep sleep, and when he awoke he found that the people of the land had eaten up all his crops.

Then he flew away to a place called Kapapakolea, in Moanalua, on Oahu, where he set out a new plantation. Here the same fortune befell him, and his time for sleep came upon him before his crops were fit for eating. When he awoke, his plantation had gone to waste.

Again he moves on, and this time settles in Lihue, Oahu, where for the third time he sets out a plantation of food, but is prevented from eating it by another interval of sleep. Awakening, he finds his crops overripe and wasted by neglect and decay.

His restless ambition now carries him to Lahuimalo, still on the island of Oahu, where his industry plants another crop of food. Six months pass, and he is about to eat of the fruits of his labor, when one day, on plunging into the river to bathe, he falls into his customary trance, and his lifeless body is floated by the stream out into the ocean and finally cast up by the waters on the sands of Maeaea, a place in Waialua, Oahu.

At the same time there arrived a man from Kauai in search of a human body to offer as a sacrifice at the temple of Kahikihaunaka at Wailua, on Kauai, and having seen the corpse of Kaopele on the beach, he asks and obtains permission of the feudal lord (*Konohiki*) of Waialua to take it. Thus it happens that Kaopele is taken by canoe to the island of Kauai and placed, along with the corpse of another man, on the altar of the temple at Wailua.

There he lay until the bones of his fellow corpse had begun to fall apart. When six moons had been accomplished, at midnight there came a burst of thunder and an earthquake. Kaopele came to life, descended from the altar, and directed his steps toward a light which he saw shining through some chinks in a neighboring house. He was received by the occupants of the house with that instant and hearty hospitality which marks the Hawaiian race, and bidden to enter ("*mai, komo mai*").

Food was set before him, with which he refreshed himself. The old man who seemed to be the head of the household was so much pleased and impressed with the bearing and appearance of our hero that he forthwith sought to secure him to be the husband of his granddaughter, a beautiful girl named Makalani. Without further ado, he persuaded him to be a suitor for the hand of the girl, and while it was yet night, started off to obtain the girl's consent and to bring her back with him.

The young woman was awakened from her slumbers in the night to hear the proposition of her grandfather, who painted to her in glowing colors the manly attractions of her suitor. The suit found favor in the eyes of the girl's parents and she herself was nothing loath; but with commendable maidenly propriety she insisted that her suitor should be brought and presented to her, and that she should not first seek him.

The sun had hardly begun to lift the dew from the grass when our young hero, accompanied by the two matchmakers, was brought into the presence of his future wife. They found favor in each other's eyes, and an ardent attachment sprang up on the instant. Matters sped apace. A separate house was assigned as the residence of the young couple, and their married life began felicitously.

But the instincts of a farmer were even stronger in the breast of Kaopele than the bonds of matrimony. In the middle of the night he arose, and, leaving the sleeping form of his bride, passed out into the darkness. He went *mauka* until he came upon an extensive upland plain, where he set to work clearing and making ready for planting. This done, he collected from various quarters shoots and roots of potato, *kalo*, banana, *waoke*, *awa*, and other plants, and before day the whole plain was a plantation. After his departure his wife awoke with a start and found her husband was gone. She went into the next house, where her parents were sleeping, and, waking them, made known her loss; but they knew nothing of his whereabouts. Much perplexed, they were still debating the cause of his departure, when he suddenly returned, and to his wife's questioning, answered that he had been at work.

She gently reproved him for interrupting their bridal night with agriculture, and told him there would be time enough for that when they had lived together a while and had completed their honeymoon. "And besides," said she, "if you wish to turn your hand to agriculture, here is the plat of ground at hand in which my father works, and you need not go up to that plain where only wild hogs roam."

To this he replied: "My hand constrains me to

plant; I crave work; does idleness bring in anything?
There is profit only when a man turns the palm of his
hand to the soil: that brings in food for family and
friends. If one were indeed the son of a king he could
sleep until the sun was high in the heavens, and then
rise and find the bundles of cooked food ready for him.
But for a plain man, the only thing to do is to cultivate
the soil and plant, and when he returns from his work
let him light his oven, and when the food is cooked
let the husband and the wife crouch about the hearth
and eat together."

Again, very early on the following morning, while
his wife slept, Kaopele rose, and going to the house of
a neighbor, borrowed a fishhook with its tackle. Then,
supplying himself with bait, he went a-fishing in the
ocean and took an enormous quantity of fish. On his
way home he stopped at the house where he had borrowed the tackle and returned it, giving the man also
half of the fish. Arrived at home, he threw the load of
fish onto the ground with a thud which waked his wife
and parents.

"So you have been a-fishing," said his wife. "Thinking you had again gone to work in the field, I went up
there, but you were not there. But what an immense
plantation you have set out! Why, the whole plain
is covered."

His father-in-law said, "A fine lot of fish, my
boy."

Thus went life with them until the crops were ripe,
when one day Kaopele said to his wife, who was now
evidently with child, "If the child to be born is a boy,

name it Kalelealuaka; but if it be a girl, name it as you will, from your side of the family."

From his manner she felt uneasy and suspicious of him, and said, "Alas! do you intend to desert me?"

Then Kaopele explained to his wife that he was not really going to leave her, as men are wont to forsake their wives, but he foresaw that that was soon to happen which was habitual to him, and he felt that on the night of the morrow a deep sleep would fall upon him (*puni ka hiamoe*), which would last for six months. Therefore, she was not to fear.

"Do not cast me out nor bury me in the ground," said he. Then he explained to her how he happened to be taken from Oahu to Kauai and how he came to be her husband, and he commanded her to listen attentively to him and to obey him implicitly. Then they pledged their love to each other, talking and not sleeping all that night.

On the following day all the friends and neighbors assembled, and as they sat about, remarks were made among them in an undertone, like this, "So this is the man who was placed on the altar of the *heiau* at Wailua." And as evening fell he bade them all *aloha*, and said that he should be separated from them for six months, but that his body would remain with them if they obeyed his commands. And, having kissed his wife, he fell into the dreamful, sacred sleep of Niolokapu.

On the sixth day the father-in-law said: "Let us bury your husband, lest he stink. I thought it was to be only a natural sleep, but it is ordinary death.

Look, his body is rigid, his flesh is cold, and he does not breathe; these are the signs of death."

But Makalani protested, "I will not let him be buried; let him lie here, and I will watch over him as he commanded; you also heard his words." But in spite of the wife's earnest protests, the hard-hearted father-in-law gathered strong vines of the *koali* (convolvulus), tied them about Kaopele's feet, and attaching to them heavy stones, caused his body to be conveyed in a canoe and sunk in the dark waters of the ocean midway between Kauai and Oahu.

Makalani lived in sorrow for her husband until the birth of her child, and as it was a boy, she called his name Kalelealuaka.

PART II

When the child was about two months old the sky became overcast and there came up a mighty storm, with lightning and an earthquake. Kaopele awoke in his dark, watery couch, unbound the cords that held his feet, and by three powerful strokes raised himself to the surface of the water. He looked toward Kauai and Oahu, but love for his wife and child prevailed and drew him to Kauai.

In the darkness of night he stood by his wife's bed and, feeling for her, touched her forehead with his clammy hand. She awoke with a start, and on his making himself known she screamed with fright, "Ghost of Kaopele!" and ran to her parents. Not until a candle was lighted would she believe it to be her husband. The step-parents, in fear and shame at their heartless conduct, fled away, and never returned. From this time forth Kaopele was never again visited by a trance; his virtue had gone out from him to the boy Kalelealuaka.

When Kalelealuaka was ten years old Kaopele began to train the lad in athletic sports and to teach him all the arts of war and combat practised throughout the islands, until he had attained great proficiency in them. He also taught him the arts of running and jumping, so that he could jump either up or down a high *pali*, or run, like a waterfowl on the surface of the water. After this, one day Kalelealuaka went over to Wailua, where he witnessed the games of the chiefs. The youth spoke contemptuously of their performances as mere child's play; and when his remark was reported to the King he challenged the young man to meet him in a boxing encounter. When Kalelealuaka came into the presence of the King his royal adversary asked him what wager he brought. As the youth had nothing with him, he seriously proposed that each one should wager his own body against that of the other one. The proposal was readily accepted. The herald sounded the signal of attack, and both contestants rushed at each other. Kalelealuaka warily avoided the attack by the King, and hastened to deliver a blow which left his opponent at his mercy; and thereupon, using his privilege, he robbed the King of his life, and to the astonishment of all, carried away the body to lay as a sacrifice on the altar of the temple, hitherto uncon-secrated by human sacrifice, which he and his father Kaopele had recently built in honor of their deity.

After a time there reached the ear of Kalelealuaka a report of the great strength of a certain chief who lived in Hanalei. Accordingly, without saying anything about his intention, he went over to the valley of Hanalei. He found the men engaged in the game of throwing heavy spears at the trunk of a cocoanut-tree. As on the previous occasion, he invited a challenge by belittling their exploits, and when challenged by the chief, fearlessly proposed, as a wager, the life of one against the other. This was accepted, and the chief had the first trial. His spear hit the stem of the huge tree and made its lofty crest nod in response to the blow. It was now the turn of Kalelealuaka to hurl the spear. In anticipation of the failure of the youth and his own success, the chief took the precaution to station his guards about Kalelealuaka, to be ready to seize him on the instant. In a tone of command our hero bade the guards fall back, and brandishing his spear, stroked and polished it with his hands from'end to end; then he poised and hurled it, and to the astonishment of all, lo! the tree was shivered to pieces. On this the people raised a shout of admiration at the prowess of the youth, and declared he must be the same hero who had slain the chief at Wailua. In this way Kalelealuaka obtained a second royal sacrifice with which to grace the altar of his temple.

One clear, calm evening, as Kalelealuaka looked out to sea, he descried the island of Oahu, which is often clearly visible from Kauai, and asked his father what land that was that stood out against them. Kaopele told the youth it was Oahu; that the cape that swam out into the ocean like a waterfowl was Kaena; that the retreating contour of the coast beyond was Waianae. Thus he described the land to his son. The result was that the adventurous spirit of Kalelealuaka was fired to explore this new island for himself, and he expressed this wish to his father. Everything that Kalelealuaka said or did was good in the eye of his father, Kaopele. Accordingly, he immediately set to work and soon had a canoe completely fitted out, in which Kalelealuaka might start on his travels. Kalelealuaka took with him, as travelling companion, a mere lad named Kaluhe, and embarked in his canoe. With two strokes of the paddle his prow grated on the sands of Waianae.

Before leaving Kauai his father had imparted to Kalelealuaka something of the topography of Oahu, and had described to him the site of his former plantation at Keahumoe. At Waianae the two travellers were treated affably by the people of the district. In reply to the questions put them, they said they were going sight-seeing. As they went along they met a party of boys amusing themselves with darting arrows; one of them asked permission to join their party. This was given, and the three turned inland and journeyed till they reached a plain of soft, whitish rock, where they all refreshed themselves with food. Then they kept on ascending, until Keahumoe lay before them, dripping with hoary moisture from the mist of the mountain, yet as if smiling through its tears. Here were standing bananas with ripened, yellow fruit, upland kalo, and sugar cane, rusty and crooked with age, while the sweet potatoes had crawled out of the earth and were cracked and dry. It was the very place where Kaopele, the father of Kalelealuaka, had years before set out the plants from which these were descended.

"This is our food, and a good place, perhaps, for us to settle down," said Kalelealuaka; "but before we make up our minds to stay here let me dart an arrow; and if it drops soon we shall stay, but if it flies afar we shall not tarry here." Kalelealuaka darted his arrow, while his companions looked on intently. The arrow flew along, passing over many a hill and valley, and finally rested beyond Kekuapoi, while they followed the direction of its wonderful flight. Kalelealuaka sent his companions on to find the arrow, telling them at the same time to go to the villages and get some awa roots for drink, while he would remain there and put up a shelter for them.

On their way the two companions of Kalelealuaka encountered a number of women washing kalo in a stream, and on asking them if they had seen their arrow flying that way they received an impertinent answer; whereupon they called out the name of the arrow, "Pua-ne, Pua-ne," and it came to their hands at once. At this the women ran away, frightened at the marvel.

The two boys then set to gathering awa roots, as they had been bidden. Seeing them picking up worthless fragments, a kind-hearted old man, who turned out to be the konohiki of the land, sent by his servants an abundance of good food to Kalelealuaka.

On their return the boys found, to their astonishment, that during their absence Kalelealuaka had put up a fine, large house, which was all complete but the mats to cover the floors. The kind-hearted *konohiki* remarked this, and immediately sent his servants to fetch mats for the floors and sets of kapa for bedding, adding the command, "And with them bring along some *malos*" (girdles used by the males). Soon all their wants were supplied, and the three youths were set up in housekeeping. To these services the kono-hiki, through his attendants, added still others; some chewed and strained the awa, while others cooked and spread for them a bountiful repast. The three youths ate and drank, and under the drowsy influence of the awa they slept until the little birds that peopled the wilderness about them waked them with their morning songs; then they roused and found the sun already climbing the heavens.

Now, Kalelealuaka called to his comrades, and said, "Rouse up and let us go to cultivating." To this they agreed, and each one set to work in his own way, work-ing his own piece of ground. The ground prepared by Kalelealuaka was a strip of great length, reaching from the mountain down toward the ocean. This he cleared and planted the same day. His two companions, how-ever, spent several days in clearing their ground, and then several days more in planting it. While these youths occupied their mountain home, the people of that region were well supplied with food. The only lack of Kalelealuaka and his comrades was animal food (literally, fish), but they supplied its place as well as they could with such herbs as the tender leaves of the popolo, which they cooked like spinach, and with inamona made from the roasted nuts of the kukui tree (*Aleurites molluccana*).

One day, as they were eking out their frugal meal with a mess of popolo cooked by the lad from Waianae, Kalelealuaka was greatly disgusted at seeing a worm in that portion that the youth was eating, and thereupon nicknamed him *Keinohoomanawanui* (sloven, or more literally, the persistently unclean). The name ever after stuck to him. This same fellow had the misfortune, one evening, to injure one of his eyes by the explosion of a kukui nut which he was roasting on the fire. As a result, that member was afflicted with soreness, and finally became blinded. But their life agreed with them, and the youths throve and increased in stature, and grew to be stout and lusty young men.

Now, it happened that ever since their stay at their mountain house, *Lelepua* (arrow flight), they had kept a torch burning all night, which was seen by Kakuhihewa, the King of Oahu, and had caused him uneasiness.

One fine evening, when they had eaten their fill and had gone to bed, Kalelealuaka called to Keinohoomanawanui and said, "Halloo there! are you asleep?"

And he replied, "No; have I drunk awa? I am restless. My eyes will not close."

"Well," said Kalelealuaka, "when you are restless at night, what does your mind find to do?"

"Nothing," said the Sloven.

"I find something to think about," said Kalelealuaka.

"What is that?" said the Sloven.

"Let us wish" (*kuko*, literally, to lust), said Kalelealuaka.

"What shall we wish?" said the Sloven.

"Whatever our hearts most earnestly desire;" said Kalelealuaka. Thereupon they both wished. The Sloven, in accordance with his nature, wished for things to eat,—the eels, from the fish-pond of Hanaloa (in the district of Ewa), to be cooked in an oven together with sweet potatoes, and a bowl of awa.

"Pshaw, what a beggarly wish!" said Kalelealuaka. "I thought you had a real wish. I have a genuine wish. Listen: The beautiful daughters of Kakuhihewa to be my wives; his fatted pigs and dogs to be baked for us; his choice kalo, sugar cane, and bananas to be served up for us; that Kakuhihewa himself send and get timber and build a house for us; that he pull the famous awa of Kahauone; that the King send and fetch us to him; that he chew the awa for us in his own mouth, strain and pour it for us, and give us to drink until we are happy, and then take us to our house."

Trembling with fear at the audacious ambition of his concupiscent companion, the Sloven replied, "If your wish should come to the ears of the King, we shall die; indeed, we should die."

In truth, as they were talking together and uttering their wishes, Kakuhihewa had arrived, and was all the time listening to their conversation from the outside of their house. When the King had heard their conversation he thrust his spear into the ground outside the inclosure about Kalelealuaka's house, and by the spear placed his stone weapon (*pahoa*), and immediately returned to his residence at Puuloa. Upon his arrival at home that night King Kakuhihewa commanded his stewards to prepare a feast, and then summoned his chiefs and table companions and said, "Let us sup." When all was ready and they had seated themselves, the King said, "Shall we eat, or shall we talk?"

One of them replied: "If it please the King, perhaps it were better for him to speak first; it may be what he has to say touches a matter of life and death; therefore, let him speak and we will listen."

Then Kakuhihewa told them the whole story of the light seen in the mountains, and of the wishes of Kalelealuaka and the Sloven.

Then up spoke the soldiers, and said: "Death! This man is worthy to be put to death; but as for the other one, let him live."

"Hold," said the King, "not so fast! Before condemning him to death, I will call together the wise men, priests, wizards, and soothsayers; perchance they will find that this is the man to overcome Kualii in battle." Thereupon all the wise men, priests, wizards, and soothsayers were immediately summoned, and after the King had explained the whole story to them they agreed with the opinion of the soldiers. Again the King interposed delay, and said, "Wait until my wise kahuna Napuaikamao comes; if his opinion agrees with yours, then, indeed, let the man be put to death; but if he is wiser than you, the man shall live. But you will have eaten this food in vain."

So the King sent one of his fleetest runners to go and fetch Napuaikamao. To him the King said, "I have sent for you to decide what is just and right in the case of these two men who lived up in the region of Waipio." Then he went on to state the whole case to this wise man.

"In regard to Keinohoomanawanui's wish," said the wise man, "that is an innocent wish, but it is profitless and will bring no blessing." At the narration of Kalelealuaka's wish he inclined his head, as if in thought; then lifting his head, he looked at the King and said: "O King, as for this man's wish, it is an ambition which will bring victory to the government. Now, then, send all your people and fetch house-timber and awa."

As soon as the wise man had given this opinion, the King commanded his chief marshal, Maliuhaaino, to set every one to work to carry out the directions of this counsellor. This was done, and before break of day every man, woman, and child in the district of Ewa, a great multitude, was on the move.

Now, when the Sloven awoke in the morning and went out of doors, he found the stone weapon (*pahoa*) of the King, with his spear, standing outside of the house. On seeing this he rushed back into the house and exclaimed to his comrades, "Alas! our wishes have been overheard by the King; here are his hatchet and his spear. I said that if the King heard us we should die, and he has indeed heard us. But yours was the fatal ambition; mine was only an innocent wish."

Even while they were talking, the babble of the

multitude drew near, and the Sloven exclaimed, "Our death approaches!"

Kalelealuaka replied, "That is not for our death; it is the people coming to get timber for our houses." But the fear of the Sloven would not be quieted.

The multitude pressed on, and by the time the last of them had reached the mountain the foremost had returned to the sea-coast and had begun to prepare the foundations for the houses, to dig the holes for the posts, to bind on the rafters and the small poles on which they tied the thatch, until the houses were done.

Meantime, some were busy baking the pigs and the poi-fed dogs in ovens; some in bringing the eels of Kanaloa and cooking them with potatoes in an oven by themselves.

The houses are completed, everything is ready, the grand marshal, Maliuhaaino, has just arrived in front of the house of the ambitious youth Kalelealuaka, and calls out "Keinohoomanawanui, come out!" and he comes out, trembling. "Kalelealuaka, come out!" and he first sends out the boy Kaluhe and then comes forth himself and stands outside, a splendid youth. The marshal stands gazing at him in bewilderment and admiration. When he has regained his equanimity he says to him, "Mount on my back and let us go down."

"No," said Kalelealuaka, "I will go by myself, and do you walk ahead. I will follow after; but do not look behind you, lest you die."

As soon as they had started down, Kalelealuaka was transported to Kuaikua, in Helemano. There he plunged into the water and bathed all over ; this done, he called on his ancestral shades (*Aumakua*), who came and performed on him the rite of circumcision while lightning flashed, thunder sounded, and the earth quaked.

Kaopele, on Kauai, heard the commotion and exclaimed, "Ah! my son has received the purifying rite—the offspring of the gods goes to meet the sovereign of the land" (*Alii aimoku*).

Meanwhile, the party led by Maliuhaaino was moving slowly down toward the coast, because the marshal himself was lame. Returning from his purification, Kalelealuaka alighted just to the rear of the party, who had not noticed his absence, and becoming impatient at the tedious slowness of the journey,—for the day was waning, and the declining sun was already standing over a peak of the Waianae Mountains called Puukuua,—this marvellous fellow caught up the lame marshal in one hand and his two comrades in the other, and, flying with them, set them down at Puuloa. But the great marvel was, that they knew nothing about being transported, yet they had been carried and set down as from a sheet.

On their arrival at the coast all was ready, and the people were waiting for them. A voice called out, "Here is you house, Keinohoomanawanui!" and the Sloven entered with alacrity and found bundles of his wished-for eels and potatoes already cooked and awaiting his disposal.

But Kalelealuaka proudly declined to enter the house prepared for himself when the invitation came

to him, "Come in! this is your house," all because his
little friend Kaluhe, whose eyes had often been filled
with smoke while cooking *luau* and roasting kukui
nuts for him, had not been included in the invitation,
and he saw that no provision had been made for him.
When this was satisfactorily arranged Kalelealuaka
and his little friend entered and sat down to eat.   The
King, with his own hand, poured out awa for Kalelealuaka, brought him a gourd of water to rinse his
mouth, offered him food, and waited upon him till he
had supplied all his wants.

Now, when Kalelealuaka had well drunken, and was
beginning to feel drowsy from the awa, the lame
marshal came in and led him to the two daughters of
Kakuhihewa, and from that time these two lovely girls
were his wives.

PART III

Thus they lived for perhaps thirty days (*he mau
anahulu*), when a messenger arrived, announcing that
Kualii was making war at Moanalua.   The soldiers
of Kakuhihewa quickly made themselves ready, and
among them Keinohoomanawanui went out to battle.
The lame marshal had started for the scene the night
before.

On the morning of the day of battle, Kalelealuaka
said to his wives that he had a great hankering for
some shrimps and moss, which must be gathered in a
particular way, and that nothing else would please his
appetite.   Thereupon, they dutifully set out to obtain
these things for him.   As soon as they had gone from

the house Kalelealuaka flew to Waianae and arrayed himself with wreaths of the fine-leaved *maile* (*Maile laulii*), which is peculiar to that region. Thence he flew to Napeha, where the lame marshal, Maliuhaaino, was painfully climbing the hill on his way to battle. Kalelealuaka cheerily greeted him, and the following dialogue occurred:

K. "Whither are you trudging, Maliuhaaino?"

M. "What! don't you know about the war?"

K. "Let me carry you."

M. "How fast you travel! Where are you from?"

K. "From Waianae."

M. "So I see from your wreaths. Yes, carry me, and Waianae shall be yours."

At the word Kalelealuaka picked up the cripple and set him down on an eminence *mauka* of the battle-field, saying, "Remain you here and watch me. If I am killed in the fight, you return by the same way we came and report to the King."

Kalelealuaka then addressed himself to the battle, but before attacking the enemy he revenged himself on those who had mocked and jeered at him for not joining the forces of Kakuhihewa. This done, he turned his hand against the enemy, who at the time were advancing and inflicting severe loss in the King's army.

To what shall we compare the prowess of our hero? A man was plucked and torn in his hand as if he were but a leaf. The commotion in the ranks of the enemy was as when a powerful waterfowl lashes the water with his wings (*O haehae ka manu, Ke ale nei ka*

wai).   Kalelealuaka moved forward in his work of
destruction until he had slain the captain who stood
beside the rebel chief, Kualii.   From the fallen captain he took his feather cloak and helmet and cut
off his right ear and the little finger of his right hand.
Thus ended the slaughter that day.

The enthusiasm of the cripple was roused to the
highest pitch on witnessing the achievements of Kalelealuaka, and he determined to return and report that
he had never seen his equal on the battlefield.

Kalelealuaka returned to Puuloa and hid the feather
cloak and helmet under the mats of his bed, and having fastened the dead captain's ear and little finger to
the side of the house, lay down and slept.

After a while, when the two women, his wives,
returned with the moss and shrimps, he complained
that the moss was not gathered as he had directed,
and that they had been gone such a long time that his
appetite had entirely left him, and he would not eat
of what they had brought.   At this the elder sister
said nothing, but the younger one muttered a few
words to herself; and as they were all very tired they
soon went to sleep.

They had slept a long while when the tramp of the
soldiers of Kakuhihewa was heard, returning from the
battle.   The King immediately asked how the battle
had gone.   The soldiers answered that the battle had
gone well, but that Keinohoomanawanui alone had
greatly distinguished himself.   To this the King replied
he did not believe that the Sloven was a great warrior,
but when the cripple returned he would learn the truth.

About midnight the footsteps of the lame marshal were heard outside of the King's house. Kakuhihewa called to him, "Come, how went the battle?"

"Can't you have patience and let me take breath?" said the marshal. Then when he had rested himself he answered, "They fought, but there was one man who excelled all the warriors in the land. He was from Waianae. I gave Waianae to him as a reward for carrying me."

"It shall be his," said the King.

"He tore a man to pieces," said the cripple, "as he would tear a banana-leaf. The champion of Kualii's army he killed, and plundered him of his feather cloak and helmet."

"The soldiers say that Keinohoomanawanui was the hero of the day," said the King.

"What!" said the cripple. "He did nothing. He merely strutted about. But this man — I never saw his equal; he had no spear, his only weapons were his hands; if a spear was hurled at him, he warded it off with his hair. His hair and features, by the way, greatly resemble those of your son-in-law."

Thus they conversed till daybreak.

After a few days, again came a messenger announcing that the rebel Kualii was making war on the plains of Kulaokahua. On hearing this Kakuhihewa immediately collected his soldiers. As usual, the lame marshal set out in advance the evening before the battle.

In the morning, after the army had gone, Kalelealuaka said to his wives, "I am thirsting for some water taken with the snout of the calabash held downward. I shall not relish it if it is taken with the snout turned up." Now, Kalelealuaka knew that they could not fill the calabash if held this way, but he resorted to this artifice to prevent the two young women from knowing of his miraculous flight to the battle. As soon as the young women had got out of sight he hastened to Waialua and arrayed himself in the rough and shaggy wreaths of *uki* from the lagoons of Ukoa and of *hinahina* from Kealia. Thus arrayed, he alighted behind the lame marshal as he climbed the hill at Napeha, slapped him on the back, exchanged greetings with him, and received a compliment on his speed; and when asked whence he came, he answered from Waialua. The shrewd, observant cripple recognized the wreaths as being those of Waialua, but he did not recognize the man, for the wreaths with which Kalelealuaka had decorated himself were of such a color — brownish gray — as to give him the appearance of a man of middle age. He lifted the cripple as before, and set him down on the brow of Puowaina (Punch Bowl Hill), and received from the grateful cripple, as a reward for his service, all the land of Waialua for his own.

This done, Kalelealuaka repeated the performances of the previous battle. The enemy melted away before him, whichever way he turned. He stayed his hand only when he had slain the captain of the host and stripped him of his feather cloak and helmet, taking also his right ear and little finger. The speed with which Kalelealuaka returned to his home at Puuloa was like the flight of a bird. The spoils and trophies of this battle he disposed of as before.

The two young women, Kalelealuaka's wives, turned the nozzle of the water-gourd downward, as they were bidden, and continued to press it into the water, in the vain hope that it might rise and fill their container, until the noonday sun began to pour his rays directly upon their heads; but no water entered their calabash. Then the younger sister proposed to the elder to fill the calabash in the usual way, saying that Kalelealuaka would not know the difference. This they did, and returned home.

Kalelealuaka would not drink of the water, declaring that it had been dipped up. At this the younger wife laughed furtively; the elder broke forth and said: "It is due to the slowness of the way you told us to employ in getting the water. We are not accustomed to the menial office of fetching water; our father treated us delicately, and a man always fetched water for us, and we always used to see him pour the water into the gourd with the nozzle turned up, but you trickily ordered us to turn the nozzle down. Your exactions are heartless."

Thus the women kept complaining until, by and by, the tramp of the returning soldiers was heard, who were boasting of the great deeds of Keinohoomana-wanui. The King, however, said: "I do not believe a word of your talk; when my cripple comes he will tell me the truth. I do not believe that Keinohoo-manawanui is an athlete. Such is the opinion I have formed of him. But there is a powerful man, Kale-

lealuaka,—if he were to go into battle I am confident
he would perform wonders. Such is the opinion I
have formed of him, after careful study."

So the King waited for the return of the cripple
until night, and all night until nearly dawn. When
finally the lame marshal arrived, the King prudently
abstained from questioning him until he had rested
a while and taken breath; then he obtained from him
the whole story of this new hero from Waialua,
whose name he did not know, but who, he declared,
resembled the King's son-in-law, Kalelealuaka.

Again, on a certain day, came the report of an attack
by Kualii at Kulaokahua, and the battle was to be on
the morrow. The cripple, as usual, started off the
evening before. In the morning, Kalelealuaka called
to his wives, and said: "Where are you? Wake up.
I wish you to bake a fowl for me. Do it thus: Pluck
it; do not cut it open, but remove the inwards through
the opening behind; then stuff it with *luau* from the
same end, and bake it; by no means cut it open, lest
you spoil the taste of it."

As soon as they had left the house he flew to
Kahuku and adorned his neck with wreaths of the
pandanus fruit and his head with the flowers of the
sugar cane, thus entirely changing his appearance and
making him look like a gray-haired old man. As on
previous days, he paused behind the cripple and
greeted him with a friendly slap on the back. Then
he kindly lifted the lame man and set him down at
Puowaina. In return for this act of kindness the
cripple gave him the district of Koolau.

In this battle he first slew those soldiers in Kaku-hihewa's army who had spoken ill of him. Then he turned his hand against the warriors of Kualii, smiting them as with the stroke of lightning, and displaying miraculous powers. When he had reached the captain of Kualii's force, he killed him and despoiled his body of his feather cloak and helmet, taking also a little finger and toe. With these he flew to the cripple, whom he lifted and bore in his flight as far as Waipio, and there dropped him at a point just below where the water bursts forth at Waipahu.

Arrived at his house, Kalelealuaka, after disposing of his spoils, lay down and slept. After he had slept several hours, his wives came along in none too pleased a mood and awoke him, saying his meat was cooked. Kalelealuaka merely answered that it was so late his appetite had gone, and he did not care to eat.

At this slight his wives said: "Well, now, do you think we are accustomed to work? We ought to live without work, like a king's daughters, and when the men have prepared the food then we should go and eat it."

The women were still muttering over their grievance, when along came the soldiers, boasting of the powers of Keinohoomanawanui, and as they passed Kalelealuaka's door they said it were well if the two wives of this fellow, who lounges at home in time of war, were given to such a brave and noble warrior as Keinohoomanawanui.

The sun was just sinking below the ocean when

the footsteps of the cripple were heard at the King's door, which he entered, sitting down within. After a short time the King asked him about the battle. "The valor and prowess of this third man were even greater than those of the previous ones; yet all three resemble each other. This day, however, he first avenged himself by slaying those who had spoken ill of him. He killed the captain of Kualii's army and took his feather cloak and helmet. On my return he lifted me as far as Waipahu."

In a few days again came a report that Kualii had an army at a place called Kahapaakai, in Nuuanu. Maliuhaaino immediately marshalled his forces and started for the scene of battle the same evening.

Early the next morning Kalelealuaka awakened his wives, and said to them: "Let us breakfast, but do you two eat quietly in your own house, and I in my house with the dogs; and do not come until I call you." So they did, and the two women went and breakfasted by themselves. At his own house Kalelealuaka ordered Kaluhe to stir up the dogs and keep them barking until his return. Then he sprang away and lighted at Kapakakolea, where he overtook the cripple, whom, after the usual interchange of greetings, he lifted, and set down at a place called Waolani.

On this day his first action was to smite and slay those who had reviled him at his own door. That done, he made a great slaughter among the soldiers of Kualii; then, turning, he seized Keinohoomana-wanui, threw him down and asked him how he became blinded in one eye.

"It was lost," said the Sloven, "from the thrust of a spear, in a combat with Olopana."

"Yes, to be sure," said Kalelealuaka, "while you and I were living together at Wailuku, you being on one side of the stream and I on the other, a kukui nut burst in the fire, and that was the spear that put out your eye."

When the Sloven heard this, he hung his head. Then Kalelealuaka seized him to put him to death, when the spear of the Sloven pierced the fleshy part of Kalelealuaka's left arm, and in plucking it out the spear-head remained in the wound.

Kalelealuaka killed Keinohoomanawanui and beheaded him, and, running to the cripple, laid the trophy at his feet with the words: "I present you, Maliuhaaino, with the head of Keinohoomanawanui." This done, he returned to the battle, and went on slaying until he had advanced to the captain of Kualii's forces, whom he killed and spoiled of his feather cloak and helmet.

When Kualii saw that his chief captain, the bulwark of his power, was slain, he retreated and fled up Nuuanu Valley, pursued by Kalelealuaka, who overtook him at the head of the valley. Here Kualii surrendered himself, saying: "Spare my life. The land shall all go to Kakuhihewa, and I will dwell on it as a loyal subject under him and create no disturbance as long as I live."

To this the hero replied: "Well said! I spare your life on these terms. But if you at any time foment a rebellion, I will take your life! So, then, return, and live quietly at home and do not stir up any war in Koolau." Thus warned, Kaulii set out to return to the "deep blue palis of Koolau."

While the lame marshal was trudging homeward, bearing the head of the Sloven, Kalelealuaka alighted from his flight at his house, and having disposed in his usual manner of his spoils, immediately called to his wives to rejoin him at his own house.

The next morning, after the sun was warm, the cripple arrived at the house of the King in a state of great excitement, and was immediately questioned by him as to the issue of the battle. "The battle was altogether successful," said the marshal, "but Keinohoomanawanui was killed. I brought his head along with me and placed it on the altar *mauka* of Kalawao. But I would advise you to send at once your fleetest runners through Kona and Koolau, commanding everybody to assemble in one place, that I may review them and pick out and vaunt as the bravest that one whom I shall recognize by certain marks—for I have noted him well: he is wounded in the left arm."

Now, Kakuhihewa's two swiftest runners (*kukini*) were Keakealani and Kuhelemoana. They were so fleet that they could compass Oahu six times in a forenoon, or twelve times in a whole day. These two were sent to call together all the men of the King's domain. The men of Waianae came that same day and stood in review on the sandy plains of Puuloa. But among them all was not one who bore the marks sought for. Then came the men of Kona, of Waialua, and of Koolau, but the man was not found.

Then the lame marshal came and stood before the King and said: "Your bones shall rest in peace, Kalani. You had better send now and summon your son-in-law to come and stand before me; for he is the man." Then Kakuhihewa arose and went himself to the house of his son-in-law, and called to his daughters that he had come to get their husband to go and stand before Maliuhaaino.

Then Kalelealuaka lifted up the mats of his bed and took out the feather cloaks and the helmets and arrayed his two wives, and Kaluhe, and himself. Putting them in line, he stationed the elder of his wives first, next to her the younger, and third Kaluhe, and placing himself at the rear of the file, he gave the order to march, and thus accompanied he went forth to obey the King's command.

The lame marshal saw them coming, and in ecstasy he prostrated himself and rolled over in the dust. "The feather cloak and the helmet on your elder daughter are the ones taken from the captain of Kualii's army in the first day's fight; those on your second daughter from the captain of the second day's fight; while those on Kalelealuaka himself are from the captain killed in the battle on the fourth day. You will live, but perhaps I shall die, since he is weary of carrying me."

The lame marshal went on praising and eulogizing Kalelealuaka as he drew near. Then addressing the hero, he said: "I recognize you, having met you before. Now show your left arm to the King and to this whole assembly, that they may see where you were wounded by the spear."

Then Kalelealuaka bared his left arm and displayed his wound to the astonished multitude. Thereupon Kakuhihewa said: "Kalelealuaka and my daughters, do you take charge of the kingdom, and I will pass into the ranks of the common people under you."

After this a new arrangement of the lands was made, and the country had peace until the death of Kakuhihewa; Kalelealuaka also lived peacefully until death took him.

X

STORIES OF THE MENEHUNES

HAWAII THE ORIGINAL HOME OF THE BROWNIES

THOS. G. THRUM

STUDENTS of Hawaiian folk-lore find much of coincident interest with traditional or more historic beliefs of other and older lands. The same applies, in a measure, to some of the ancient customs of the people. This is difficult to account for, more especially since the Hawaiians possessed no written language by which such knowledge could be preserved or transmitted. Fornander and others discovered in the legends of this people traces of the story of the Flood, the standing still of the sun, and other narratives of Bible history, which some savants accept as evidence of their Aryan origin. This claim we are not disposed to dispute, but desire to present another line of tradition that has been neglected hitherto, yet has promise of much interest.

It will doubtless interest some readers to learn that Hawaii is the real home of the Brownies, or was; and that this adventurous nomadic tribe were known to the Hawaiians long before Swift's satirical mind conceived his Lilliputians.

It would be unreasonable to expect so great a range

of nationalities and peculiar characteristics among the
pygmies of Hawaii as among the Brownies of story.
Tradition naturally represents them as of one race,
and all nimble workers; not a gentleman dude, or
policeman in the whole lot.   Unlike the inquisitive
and mischievous athletes of present fame, the original
and genuine Brownies, known as the Menehunes, are
referred to as an industrious race.   In fact, it was their
alleged power to perform a marvellous amount of
labor in a short space of time that has fixed them in
the minds of Hawaiians, many of whom point to certain traces of their work in various parts of the islands
to substantiate the traditional claim of their existence.

Meeting thus with occasional references to this
active race, but mostly in a vague way, it has been a
matter of interesting inquiry among Hawaiians, some
of whom were noted *kaao*, or legend-bearers, for
further knowledge on the subject.   Very naturally
their ideas differ respecting the Menehunes.   Some
treat the subject with gravity and respect, and express
the belief that they were the original inhabitants of
these islands, but gradually gave way to the heavier-
bodied ancestors of the present race; others consider
that the history of the race has been forgotten through
the lapse of ages; while the more intelligent and better
educated look upon the Menehunes as a mythical class
of gnomes or dwarfs, and the account of their exploits
as having been handed down by tradition for social
entertainment, as other peoples relate fairy stories.

In the Hawaiian legend of Kumuhonua, Fornander
states that the Polynesians were designated as "the

people, descendants from Menehune, son of Lua Nuu, etc. It disappeared as a national name so long ago, however, that subsequent legends have changed it to a term of reproach, representing them at times as a separate race, and sometimes as a race of dwarfs, skilful laborers, but artful and cunning."

In the following account and selection of stories gathered from various native sources, as literal a rendition as possible has been observed by the translators for the better insight it gives of Hawaiian thought and character.

MOKE MANU'S ACCOUNT

The Menehunes were supposed to have been a wonderful people, small of stature and of great activity. They were always united in doing any service required of them. It was their rule that any work undertaken must be completed in one night, otherwise it would be left unfinished, as they did not labor twice on the same work; hence the origin of the saying: "*He po hookahi, a ao ua pau,*"—in one night, and by dawn it is finished.

There is no reliable history of the Menehunes. No one knows whence they came, though tradition says they were the original people of the Hawaiian Islands. They are thought to have been supernatural beings, governed by some one higher in rank than themselves, whom they recognized as having power and authority over them, that assigned them to the mountains and hills where they lived permanently. They were said to be the only inhabitants of the islands up to the time of Papa and Wakea, and were invisible to every one but their own descendants, or those connected with them in some way. Many persons could hear the noise and hum of their voices, but the gift of seeing them with the naked eye was denied to those not akin to them. They were always willing to do the bidding of their descendants, and their supernatural powers enabled them to perform some wonderful works.

PI'S WATERCOURSE

Pi was an ordinary man living in Waimea, Kauai, who wanted to construct a *mano*, or dam, across the Waimea River and a watercourse therefrom to a point near Kikiaola. Having settled upon the best locations for his proposed work, he went up to the mountains and ordered all the Menehunes that were living near Puukapele to prepare stones for the dam and watercourse. The Menehunes were portioned off for the work; some to gather stones, and others to cut them. All the material was ready in no time (*manawa ole*), and Pi settled upon the night when the work was to be done. When the time came he went to the point where the dam was to be built, and waited. At the dead of night he heard the noise and hum of the voices of the Menehunes on their way to Kikiaola, each of whom was carrying a stone. The dam was duly constructed, every stone fitting in its proper place, and the stone *auwai*, or watercourse, also laid around the bend of Kikiaola. Before the break of day the work was completed, and the water of the

Waimea River was turned by the dam into the watercourse on the flat lands of Waimea.

When the work was finished Pi served out food for the Menehunes, which consisted of shrimps (*opae*), this being the only kind to be had in sufficient quantity to supply each with a fish to himself. They were well supplied and satisfied, and at dawn returned to the mountains of Puukapele rejoicing, and the hum of their voices gave rise to the saying, *"Wawa ka Menehune i Puukapele, ma Kauai, puoho ka manu o ka loko o Kawainui ma Koolaupoko, Oahu"*—the hum of the voices of the Menehunes at Puukapele, Kauai, startled the birds of the pond of Kawainui, at Koolaupoko, Oahu.

The *auwai*, or watercourse, of Pi is still to be seen at Kikiaola.

At one time Pi also told the Menehunes to wall in a fish-pond at the bend of the Huleia River. They commenced work toward midnight, but at dawn the walls of the pond were not sufficiently finished to meet, so it was left incomplete, and has remained so to this day.

LAKA'S ADVENTURE

Wahieloa, a chief, lived at Kalaikoi, Kipahulu, Maui. He took to him a wife named Hinahawea. In due time a boy was born to them, whom Hinahowana, the mother of Hinahawea, brought up under her own care at Alaenui. She called him Laka-a-wahieloa. He was greatly petted by his parents. One day his father went to Hawaii in search of the *Ala-Koiula a Kane* for a toy for his son, landing at Punaluu, Kau, Hawaii, where he was killed in a cave called Keana-a-Kaualehu.

After a long absence Laka asked for his father, and his mother referred him to his grandmother, who, on being questioned, told him that his father went to Hawaii, and was supposed to be dead. Laka then asked for means by which he could search for his father.

His grandmother replied: "Go to the mountains and look for the tree that has leaves shaped like the moon on the night of Hilo, or Hoaka; such is the tree for a canoe."

Laka followed this advice, and went to the mountains to find the tree for his canoe. Finding a suitable one, he commenced to cut in the morning, and by sundown he had felled it to the ground. This accomplished, he went home. Returning the next day, to his surprise he could not find his fallen tree, so he cut down another, with the same result. Laka was thus tricked for several days, and in his perplexity consulted again with his grandmother, who sent him off with the same advice as before, to look for the crescent-shaped leaf.

He went to the mountains again and found the desired tree, but before cutting it he dug a big hole on the side where the Kalala-Kamahele would fall. Upon cutting the tree it fell right into the hole or trench, as designed; then he jumped into it and lay in waiting for the person or persons who were reërecting the trees he had cut down for his canoe.

While thus waiting, he heard some one talking about raising the tree and returning it to its former position, followed by some one chanting as follows:

> *E ka mano o ke Akua,*
> *Ke kini o ke Akua,*
> *Ka lehu o ke Akua,*
> *Ka lalani Akua,*
> *Ka pukui Akua!*
> *E na Akua o ke kuahiwi nei,*
> *I ka mauna,*
> *I ke kualono,*
> *I ka manowai la-e,*
> *E-iho!* [1]

When this appeal ended there was a hum and noise, and in a short time (*manawa ole*) the place was filled with a band of people, who endeavored to lift the tree; but it would not move. Laka then jumped out from his place of hiding and caught hold of two of the men, Mokuhalii and Kapaaikee, and threatened to kill them for raising again the trees he had cut for his canoe. Mokuhalii then told Laka that if they were killed, nobody would be able to make a canoe for him, nor would anybody pull it to the beach, but if they were spared they would willingly do it for him, provided Laka would first build a big and long shed (*halau*) of sufficient size to hold the canoe, and prepare sufficient food for the men. Laka gladly consenting, released them and returned to his home and built a shed on

[1] O the four thousand gods,
The forty thousand gods,
The four hundred thousand gods,
The file of gods,
The assembly of gods !
O gods of these woods,
Of the mountain,
And the knoll,
At the water-dam,
Oh, come !

the level ground of Puhikau. Then he went up to the woods and saw the canoe, ready and complete. The Menehunes told Laka that it would be brought to the halau that night. At the dead of night the hum of the voices of the Menehunes was heard; this was the commencement of the lifting of the canoe. It was not dragged, but held up by hand. The second hum of voices brought the canoe to Haloamekiei, at Pueo. And at the third hum the canoe was carefully laid down in the halau. Food and fish were there spread out for the workers, the *ha* of the taro for food, and the opae and oopu for fish. At dawn the Menehunes returned to their home. Kuahalau was the name of the halau, the remains of the foundation of which were to be seen a few years ago, but now it is ploughed over. The hole dug by Laka still exists.

KEKUPUA'S CANOE

Kakae, a chief, lived at Wahiawa, Kukaniloko, Waialua, Oahu. One day his wife told him that she desired to go in search of her brother, Kahanaiakeakua, who was supposed to be living at Tahiti. Kakae thereupon ordered his man Kekupua to go into the woods and find a suitable tree and make a canoe for his wife for this foreign voyage. Kekupua, with a number of men under him, searched in the forest belt of Wahiawa, Helemano, and Waoala, as also through the woods of Koolau, without success. From Kahana they made a search through the mountains till they came to Kilohana, in Kalihi Valley, and from there to Waolani, in Nuuanu, where they slept in a cave.

In the dead of night they heard the hum as of human voices, but were unable to discern any person, though the voices sounded close to them. At dawn silence reigned again, and when the sun arose, lo, and behold! there stood a large mound of stones, the setting of which resembled that of a *heiau*, or temple, the remains of which are said to be noticeable to this day.

Kekupua and his men returned to their chief and reported their unsuccessful search for a suitable *koa* (*Acacia koa*) tree for the desired canoe, and related also the incident at Waolani. Kakae, being a descendant of the Menehunes, knew immediately the authors of the strange occurrence. He therefore instructed Kekupua to proceed to Makaho and Kamakela and to stay there till the night of Kane, then go up to Puunui and wait till hearing the hum and noise of the Menehunes, which would be the signal of their finishing the canoe. And thus it was; the Menehunes, having finished the canoe, were ready to pull it to the sea. He directed them to look sharp, and two men would be noticed holding the ropes at the *pu* (or head) of the canoe. One of them would leap from one side to the other; he was the director of the work and was called *pale*. There would be some men farther behind, holding the *kawelewele*, or guiding-ropes. They were the *kahunas* that superintended the construction of the canoe. He reminded them to remember these directions, and when they saw these men, to give them orders and show them the course to take in pulling the canoe to the sea.

Kekupua followed all these instructions faithfully.

He waited at Puunui till dusk, when he heard a hum as of many voices, and proceeding farther up near the slope of Alewa he saw these wonderful people. They were like ordinary human beings but diminutive. He directed them to pull the canoe along the *nae*, or farther side of the Puunui stream. By this course the canoe was brought down as far as Kaalaa, near Waikahalulu, where, when daylight came, they left their burden and returned to Waolani. The canoe was left in the ditch, where it remained for many generations, and was called Kawaa-a-Kekupua (Kekupua's canoe), in honor of the servant of the chief Kakae.

Thus, even with the help of the Menehunes, the wife of Kakae was not satisfied in her desire.

AS HEIAU BUILDERS

The Menehunes are credited with the construction of numerous *heiaus* (ancient temples) in various parts of the islands.

The heiau of Mookini, near Honoipu, Kohala, is pointed out as an instance of their marvellous work. The place selected for the site of the temple was on a grassy plain. The stones in the nearest neighborhood were for some reason not deemed suitable for the work, so those of Pololu Valley, distant some twelve miles, were selected. Tradition says the Menehunes were placed in a line covering the entire distance from Pololu to Honoipu, whereby the stones were passed from hand to hand for the entire work. Work was begun at the quiet of night, and at cockcrow in the morning it was finished. Thus in one night the heiau of Mookini was built.

Another temple of their erection was at Pepeekeo, Hilo, the peculiarity of the work being that the stones had been brought together by the residents of that part of the district, by direction of the chief, but that in one night, the Menehunes gathered together and built it. The chief and his people were surprised on coming the next morning to resume their labors, to find the heiau completed.

There stands on the pali of Waikolu, near Kalau-papa, Molokai, a heiau that Hawaiians believe to have been constructed by no one else than the Menehunes. It is on the top of a ledge in the face of a perpendicular cliff, with a continuous inaccessible cliff behind it reaching hundreds of feet above. No one has ever been able to reach it either from above or from below; and the marvel is how the material, which appears to be seashore stones, was put in place.

XI

KAHALAOPUNA, PRINCESS OF MANOA

MRS. E. M. NAKUINA

AKAAKA (laughter) is a projecting spur of the
mountain range at the head of Manoa Valley,
forming the ridge running back to and above Waiakeakua, "the water of the gods." Akaaka was united in
marriage to Nalehuaakaaka, still represented by some
lehua (*Metrosideros polymorpha*) bushes on the very
brow of the spur or ridge. They had two children,
twins, Kahaukani, a boy, and Kauakuahine, a girl.
These children were adopted at birth by a chief,
Kolowahi, and chiefess, Pohakukala, who were brother
and sister, and cousins of Akaaka. The brother took
charge of the boy, Kahaukani, a synonym for the
Manoa wind; and Pohakukala the girl, Kauakuahine,
meaning the famous Manoa rain. When the children
were grown up, the foster parents determined that
they should be united; and the children, having been
brought up separately and in ignorance of their rela-
tionship, made no objections. They were accordingly
married and a girl was born to them, who was called
Kahalaopuna. Thus Kolowahi and Pohakukala, by
conspiring to unite the twin brother and sister, made
permanent the union of rain and wind for which

Manoa Valley is noted; and the fruit of such a union was the most beautiful woman of her time. So the Manoa girls, foster children of the Manoa rains and winds, have generally been supposed to have inherited the beauty of Kahalaopuna.

A house was built for Kahalaopuna at Kahaiamano on the road to Waiakekua, where she lived with a few attendants. The house was surrounded by a fence of auki (*dracæna*), and a *puloulou* (sign of kapu) was placed on each side of the gate, indicative of forbidden ground. The puloulou were short, stout poles, each surmounted by a ball of white kapa cloth, and indicated that the person or persons inhabiting the premises so defined were of the highest rank, and sacred.

Kahalaopuna was very beautiful from her earliest childhood. Her cheeks were so red and her face so bright that a glow emanated therefrom which shone through the thatch of her house when she was in; a rosy light seemed to envelop the house, and bright rays seemed to play over it constantly. When she went to bathe in the spring below her house, the rays of light surrounded her like a halo. The natives maintain that this bright light is still occasionally seen at Kahaiamano, indicating that the spirit of Kahalaopuna is revisiting her old home.

She was betrothed in childhood to Kauhi, the young chief of Kailua, in Koolau, whose parents were so sensible of the honor of the contemplated union of their son with the Princess of Manoa, who was deemed of a semi-supernatural descent, that they

always sent the poi of Kailua and the fish of Kawainui for the girl's table. She was thus, as it were,
brought up entirely on the food of her prospective
husband.

When she was grown to young womanhood, she
was so exquisitely beautiful that the people of the
valley would make visits to the outer puloulou at the
sacred precinct of Luaalea, the land adjoining Kahaiamano, just to get a glimpse of the beauty as she went
to and from the spring. In this way the fame of her
surpassing loveliness was spread all over the valley,
and came to the ears of two men, Kumauna and Keawaa, both of whom were disfigured by a contraction of
the lower eyelids, and were known as *makahelei*
(drawn eyes). Neither of these men had ever seen
Kahalaopuna, but they fell in love with her from hear-
say, and not daring to present themselves to her
as suitors on account of their disfigurement, they
would weave and deck themselves *leis* (wreaths) of
maile (*Alyxia olivæformis*), ginger, and ferns and go to
Waikiki for surf-bathing. While there they would
indulge in boasting of their conquest of the famous
beauty, representing the leis with which they were
decked as love-gifts from Kahalaopuna. Now, when
the surf of Kalehuawehe at Waikiki was in proper
condition, it would attract people from all parts of the
island to enjoy the delightful sport. Kauhi, the
betrothed of Kahalaopuna, was one of these. The
time set for his marriage to Kahalaopuna was drawing
near, and as yet he had not seen her, when the assertions of the two makahelei men came to his ears.

These were repeated so frequently that Kauhi finally came to believe them, and they so filled him with jealous rage of his betrothed that he determined to kill her. He started for Manoa at dawn, and proceeded as far as Mahinauli, in mid-valley, where he rested under a hala (*Pandanus odoratissimus*) tree that grew in the grove of wiliwili (*Erythrina monosperma*). He sat there some time, brooding over the fancied injury to himself, and nursing his wrath. Upon resuming his walk he broke off and carried along with him a bunch of hala nuts. It was quite noon when he reached Kahaiamano and presented himself before the house of Kahalaopuna. The latter had just awakened from a sleep, and was lying on a pile of mats facing the door, thinking of going to the spring, her usual bathing-place, when she perceived a stranger at the door.

She looked at him some time and, recognizing him from oft repeated descriptions, asked him to enter; but Kauhi refused, and asked her to come outside. The young girl had been so accustomed from early childhood to consider herself as belonging to Kauhi, and of being indebted to him, as it were, for her daily food, that she obeyed him unhesitatingly.

He perhaps intended to kill her then, but the girl's unhesitating obedience as well as her extreme loveliness made him hesitate for a while; and after looking intently at her for some time he told her to go and bathe and then prepare herself to accompany him in a ramble about the woods.

While Kahalaopuna was bathing, Kauhi remained

moodily seated where she had left him, and watched the bright glow, like rainbow rays, playing above the spring. He was alternately filled with jealousy, regret, and longing for the great beauty of the girl; but that did not make him relent in his dreadful purpose. He seemed to resent his betrothed's supposed infidelity the more because she had thrown herself away on such unworthy persons, who were, besides, ugly and disfigured, while he, Kauhi, was not only a person of rank and distinction, but possessed also of considerable manly beauty.

When she was ready he motioned her to follow him, and turned to go without a word. They went across Kumakaha to Hualea, when the girl said, "Why don't you stay and have something to eat before we go?"

He answered rather surlily, "I don't care to eat; I have no appetite."

He looked so sternly at her as he said this that she cried out to him, "Are you annoyed with me? Have I displeased you in any way?"

He only said, "Why, what have you done that would displease me?"

He kept on his way, she following, till they came to a large stone in Aihualama, when he turned abruptly and, facing the young girl, looked at her with an expression of mingled longing and hate. At last, with a deep sigh, he said, "You are beautiful, my betrothed, but, as you have been false, you must die."

The young girl looked up in surprise at these strange words, but saw only hatred and a deadly purpose in Kauhi's eyes; so she said: "If I have to die, why did you not kill me at home, so that my people could have buried my bones; but you brought me to the wild woods, and who will bury me? If you think I have been false to you, why not seek proof before believing it?"

But Kauhi would not listen to her appeal. Perhaps it only served to remind him of what he considered was his great loss. He struck her across the temple with the heavy bunch of hala nuts he had broken off at Mahinauli, and which he had been holding all the time. The blow killed the girl instantly, and Kauhi hastily dug a hole under the side of the rock and buried her; then he started down the valley toward Waikiki.

As soon as he was gone, a large owl, who was a god, and a relative of Kahalaopuna, and had followed her from home, immediately set to digging the body out; which done, it brushed the dirt carefully off with its wings and, breathing into the girl's nostrils, restored her to life. It rubbed its face against the bruise on the temple, and healed it immediately. Kauhi had not advanced very far on his way when he heard the voice of Kahalaopuna singing a lament for his unkindness, and beseeching him to believe her, or, at least, prove his accusation.

Hearing her voice, Kauhi returned, and, seeing the owl flying above her, recognized the means of her resurrection; and, going up to the girl, ordered her to follow him. They went up the side of the ridge which divides Manoa Valley from Nuuanu. It was hard work for the tenderly nurtured maiden to climb the steep mountain ridge, at one time through a thorny tangle of underbrush, and at another clinging against the bare face of the rocks, holding on to swinging vines for support. Kauhi never offered to assist her, but kept on ahead, only looking back occasionally to see that she followed. When they arrived at the summit of the divide she was all scratched and bruised, and her *pa-u* (skirt) in tatters. Seating herself on a stone to regain her breath, she asked Kauhi where they were going. He never answered, but struck her again with the hala branch, killing her instantly, as before. He then dug a hole near where she lay, and buried her, and started for Waikiki by way of the Kakea ridge. He was no sooner out of sight than the owl again scratched the dirt away and restored the girl, as before. Again she followed and sang a song of love and regret for her lover's anger, and pleaded with him to lay aside his unjust suspicions. On hearing her voice again, Kauhi returned and ordered her to follow him. They descended into Nuuanu Valley, at Kaniakapupu, and crossed over to Waolani ridge, where he again killed and buried the faithful girl, who was again restored by the owl. When he was on his way back, as before, she sang a song, describing the perils and difficulties of the way traversed by them, and ended by pleading for pardon for the unknown fault. The wretched man, on hearing her voice again, was very angry; and his repeated acts of cruelty and the suffering endured by the girl, far from softening his heart, only served to render him more brutal, and to extinguish what little spark of kindly feeling he might have had originally. His only thought was to kill her for good, and thus obtain some satisfaction for his wasted poi and fish. He returned to her and ordered her, as before, to follow him, and started for Kilohana, at the head of Kalihi Valley, where he again killed her. She was again restored by the owl, and made her resurrection known by singing to her cruel lover. He this time took her across gulches, ravines, and plains, until they arrived at Pohakea, on the Ewa slope of the Kaala Mountains, where he killed her and buried her under a large *koa* (*Acacia koa*) tree. The faithful owl tried to scrape the dirt away, so as to get at the body of the girl, but his claws became entangled in the numerous roots and rootlets which Kauhi had been careful not to cut away. The more the owl scratched, the more deeply tangled he got, and, finally, with bruised claws and ruffled feathers, he had to give up the idea of rescuing the girl; and perhaps he thought it useless, as she would be sure to make her resurrection known to Kauhi. So the owl left, and followed Kauhi on his return to Waikiki.

There had been another witness to Kauhi's cruelties, and that was Elepaio (*Chasiempis sandwichensis*), a little green bird, a cousin to Kahalaopuna. As soon as this bird saw that the owl had deserted the body of Kahalaopuna, it flew straight to Kahaukani and Kauakuahine, and told them of all that had happened. The girl had been missed, but, as some of the servants had recognized Kauhi, and had seen them leave together for what they supposed was a ramble in the adjoining woods, no great anxiety had been felt, as yet. But when the little bird told his tale, there was great consternation, and even positive disbelief; for, how could any one in his senses, they argued, be guilty of such cruelty to such a lovely, innocent being, and one, too, belonging entirely to himself.

In the meantime, the spirit of the murdered girl discovered itself to a party who were passing by; and one of them, a young man, moved with compassion, went to the tree indicated by the spirit, and, removing the dirt and roots, found the body, still warm. He wrapped it in his *kihei* (shoulder scarf), and then covered it entirely with maile, ferns, and ginger, and, making a *haawe*, or back-load, of it, carried it to his home at Kamoiliili. There, he submitted the body to his elder brother, who called upon two spirit sisters of theirs, with whose aid they finally succeeded in restoring it to life. In the course of the treatment she was frequently taken to an underground water-cave, called Mauoki, for the *Kakelekele* (hydropathic cure). The water-cave has ever since been known as the "Water of Kahalaopuna."

The young man who had rescued her from the grave naturally wanted her to become his bride; but the girl refused, saying that as long as Kauhi lived she was his, and none other's, as her very body was, as it were, nourished on his food, and was as much his property as the food had been.

The elder brother then counselled the younger to seek, in some way, the death of Kauhi. To this end they conspired with the parents of Kahalaopuna to keep her last resurrection secret. The young man then set to work to learn all the meles Kahalaopuna had sung to her lover during that fatal journey. When he knew these songs well, he sought the *kilu* (play, or game) houses of the King and high chiefs, where Kauhi was sure to be found.

One day, when Kauhi was playing, this young man placed himself on the opposite side, and as Kauhi ceased, took up the kilu and chanted the first of Kahalaopuna's meles.

Kauhi was very much surprised, and contrary to the etiquette of the game of kilu, stopped him in his play to ask him where he had learned that song. The young man answered he had learned it from Kahalaopuna, the famous Manoa beauty, who was a friend of his sister's and who was now on a visit at their house. Kauhi, knowing the owl had deserted the body of the girl, felt certain that she was really dead, and accused the other of telling a lie. This led to an angry and stormy scene, when the antagonists were parted by orders of the King.

The next night found them both at the kilu house, when the second of Kahalaopuna's songs was sung, and another angry discussion took place. Again they were separated by others. On the third night, the third song having been sung, the dispute between the young men became so violent that Kauhi told the young man that the Kahalaopuna he knew must be an impostor, as the real person of that name was dead, to his certain knowledge. He dared him to produce the young woman whom he had been representing as Kahalaopuna; and should she not prove to be the genuine one then his life should be the forfeit, and on the other hand, if it should be the real one, then he, Kauhi, should be declared the liar and pay for his insults to the other with his life.

This was just what the young man had been scheming to compass, and he quickly assented to the challenge, calling on the King and chiefs to take notice of the terms of agreement, and to see that they were enforced.

On the appointed day Kahalaopuna went to Waikiki, attended by her parents, relatives, servants, and the two spirit sisters, who had assumed human form for that day so as to accompany their friend and advise her in case of necessity. Akaaka, the grandfather, who had been residing in Waikiki some little time previous to the dispute between the young men, was appointed one of the judges at the approaching trial.

Kauhi had consulted the priests and sorcerers of his family as to the possibility of the murdered girl having assumed human shape for the purpose of working him some injury. Kaea, a famous priest and seer of his family, told him to have the large leaves of the a-pe (*Calladium costatum*) spread where Kahalaopuna and party were to be seated. If she was a spirit, she would not be able to tear the a-pe leaf on which she would be seated, but if human, the leaf or leaves would be torn. With the permission of the King, this was done. The latter, surrounded by the highest chiefs and a vast assemblage from all parts of the island, was there to witness the test.

When Kahalaopuna and party were on the road to the scene of the test, her spirit friends informed her of the a-pe leaves, and advised her to trample on them so as to tear them as much as possible, as they, being spirits, would be unable to tear the leaves on which they should be seated, and if any one's attention were drawn to them, they would be found out and killed by the *poe po-i uhane* (spirit catchers).

The young girl faithfully performed what was required of her. Kaea, on seeing the torn leaves, remarked that she was evidently human, but that he felt the presence of spirits, and would watch for them, feeling sure they were in some way connected with the girl. Akaaka then told him to look in a calabash of water, when he would in all probability see the spirits. The seer, in his eagerness to unravel the mystery, forgot his usual caution and ordered a vessel of water to be brought, and, looking in, he saw only his own reflection. Akaaka at that moment caught the reflection of the seer (which was his spirit), and crushed it between his palms, and at that moment the seer dropped down dead. Akaaka now turned around and opened his arms and embraced Kahalaopuna, thus acknowledging her as his own beloved granddaughter.

The King now demanded of the girl and of Kauhi an account of all that had happened between them, and of the reported death of the maiden. They both told their stories, Kauhi ascribing his anger to hearing the assertions of the two disfigured men, Kumauna and Keawaa. These two, on being confronted with the girl, acknowledged never having seen her before, and that all their words had been idle boastings. The King then said: "As your fun has cost this innocent girl so much suffering, it is my will that you two and Kauhi suffer death at once, as a matter of justice; and if your gods are powerful enough to restore you, so much the better for you."

Two large *imus* (ground ovens) had been heated by the followers of the young men, in anticipation of the possible fate of either, and Kauhi, with the two mischief-makers and such of their respective followers and retainers as preferred to die with their chiefs, were baked therein.

The greater number of Kauhi's people were so incensed with his cruelty to the lovely young girl that they transferred their allegiance to her, offering themselves for her vassals as restitution, in a measure, for the undeserved sufferings borne by her at the hands of their cruel chief.

The King gave her for a bride to the young man who had not only saved her, but had been the means of avenging her wrongs.

The imus in which Kauhi and his companions were baked were on the side of the stream of Apuakehau, in the famous Ulukou grove, and very near the sea. The night following, a great tidal wave, sent in by a powerful old shark god, a relative of Kauhi's, swept over the site of the two ovens, and in the morning it was seen that their contents had disappeared. The bones had been taken by the old shark into the sea. The chiefs, Kumauna and Keawaa, were, through the power of their family gods, transformed into the two mountain peaks on the eastern corner of Manoa Valley, while Kauhi and his followers were turned into sharks.

Kahalaopuna lived happily with her husband for about two years. Her grandfather, knowing of Kauhi's transformation, and aware of his vindictive nature, strictly forbade her from ever going into the sea. She remembered and heeded the warning during those years, but one day, her husband and all their men having gone to Manoa to cultivate kalo (*Colocasia antiquorum*), she was left alone with her maid servants.

The surf on that day was in fine sporting condition, and a number of young women were surf-riding, and Kahalaopuna longed to be with them. Forgetting the warning, as soon as her mother fell asleep she slipped out with one of her maids and swam out on a surf-board. This was Kauhi's opportunity, and as soon as she was fairly outside the reef he bit her in two and held the upper half of the body up out of the water, so that all the surf-bathers would see and know that he had at last obtained his revenge.

Immediately on her death the spirit of the young woman went back and told her sleeping mother of what had befallen her. The latter woke up, and, missing her, gave the alarm. This was soon confirmed by the terrified surf-bathers, who had all fled ashore at seeing the terrible fate of Kahalaopuna. Canoes were launched and manned, and chase given to the shark and his prey, which could be easily tracked by the blood.

He swam just far enough below the surface of the water to be visible, and yet too far to be reached with effect by the fishing-spears of the pursuers. He led them a long chase to Waianae; then, in a sandy opening in the bottom of the sea, where everything was visible to the pursuers, he ate up the young woman, so that she could never again be restored to this life.

Her parents, on hearing of her end, retired to Manoa Valley, and gave up their human life, resolving themselves into their supernatural elements. Kahaukani, the father, is known as the Manoa wind, but his usual and visible form is the grove of ha-u (*hibiscus*) trees, below Kahaiamano. Kauakuahine, the mother, assumed her rain form, and is very often to be met with about the former home of her beloved child.

The grandparents also gave up their human forms, and returned, the one to his mountain form, and the other into the lehua bushes still to be met with on the very brow of the hill, where they keep watch over the old home of their petted and adored grandchild.

XII

THE PUNAHOU SPRING

MRS. E. M. NAKUINA

THERE formerly lived on the Kaala Mountains a chief by the name of Kahaakea. He had two children, a boy and a girl, twins, whose mother had died at their birth. The brother was called *Kauawaahila* (Waahila Rain), and the girl *Kauakiowao* (Mountain Mist). Kahaakea was very tenderly attached to his motherless children, and after a while took to himself a wife, thinking thus to provide his children with a mother's care and love. This wife was called Hawea and had a boy by her former husband. This boy was deformed and ugly, while the twins were very beautiful. The stepmother was jealous of their beauty, and resented the universal admiration expressed for them, while no one noticed her boy except with looks of aversion. She was very considerate toward the twins when their father was present, but hated and detested them most violently. When they were about ten years old their father had occasion to go to Hawaii, and had to remain away a long time. He felt perfectly safe in leaving his children with his wife, as she had always feigned great love for them, and had successfully concealed from him her real feelings in regard to them.

But as soon as he was fairly away she commenced a series of petty persecutions of the poor children.

It seems the mother of the children had been "*uhae ia*" at her death. That is, certain prayers, invocations, fasting, and humiliation had been performed by certain relatives of the deceased, and quantities of prepared awa, black, unblemished pig, red fish, and all the customary food of the gods, had been prepared and offered with the object of strengthening the spirit of the departed and of attracting it strongly, as well as giving it a sort of power and control over mundane affairs and events. So when Hawea began to persecute her stepchildren, the spirit of their own mother would assist and protect them.

The persecutions of the stepmother at last became unendurable to the twins. She not only deprived them of food, clothing, and water, but subjected them besides to all sorts of indignities and humiliations. Driven to desperation, they fled to Konahuanui, the mountain peak above the Pali of Nuuanu; but were soon discovered and driven away from there by the cruel Hawea. They then went to the head of Manoa Valley. The stepmother was not at all pleased at their getting out of the way of her daily persecutions, and searched for them everywhere. She finally tracked them by the constant appearance of rainbows at the head of Manoa Valley, those unfailing attendants of rain and mist. The children were again driven away and told to return to Kaala, where they would be constantly under her eye; but they ran and hid themselves in a small cave on the side of the hill of Kukaoo,

whose top is crowned by the temple of the Menehunes. Here they lived some time and cultivated a
patch of sweet potatoes, their food at this time being
grasshoppers and greens. The greens were the leaves
and the tender shoots of the popolo, aheahea, pakai,
laulele and potato vines, cooked by rolling hot stones
around and among them in a covered gourd. This is
called the *puholoholo*.

When their potato tubers were fit to be eaten, the
brother (Waahila Rain) made a double *imu* (oven),
having a *kapu*, or sacred side, for his food and a *noa*, or
free side, for his sister. The little cave that was their
dwelling was also divided in two, a sacred and a free
part, respectively, for brother and sister. The cave can
still be seen, and the wall of stone dividing it in two
was still intact a few years ago, as also was the double
imu. In olden times it was tabooed to females to
appear at any eating-place of the males.

When their crops were fairly ripe, the stepmother
found them again, and drove them away from their
cave, she appropriating the fruit of their labors. The
children fled to the rocky hills just back of Punahou,
where they found two small caves, which the brother
and sister occupied, respectively, as dwellings. The
rolling plains and small ravines of the surrounding
country, and of what was later known as the Punahou
pasture, were not then covered with manienie grass,
but with the indigenous shrubs and bushes, tall ilimas,
aheaheas, popolo, etc., making close thickets, with
here and there open spaces covered with *manienie-
akiaki*, the valuable medicinal grass of the olden times.

These shrubs and bushes either bore edible fruit or flowers, or the leaves and tender shoots made nourishing and satisfying food when cooked in the way previously described. The poor children lived on these and grasshoppers, and sometimes wild fowl.

One day the sister, Kauakiowao, told her brother that she wanted to bathe, and complained of their having taken up their residence in a place where no water could be found. Her brother hushed her complaint by telling her that it was a safe place, and one where their stepmother would not be likely to look for them, but he would try to get her some water. In his trips around the neighborhood for fruit and greens he had noticed a large rain-water pond to the east of the hill on which they dwelt. This pond was called Kanawai. Here he sometimes came to snare wild ducks. He also had met and knew the Kakea water god, a moo, who had charge of and controlled all the water sources of Manoa and Makiki Valleys. This god was one of the ancestors of the children on the mother's side, and was on the best of terms with Waahila rain. The boy paid him a visit, and asked him to assist him to open a watercourse from the pond of Kanawai to a place he indicated in front of and below the caves inhabited by himself and his sister. The old water god not only consented to help his young relative, but promised to divide the water supply of the neighboring Wailele spring, and let it run into the watercourse that the boy would make, thus insuring its permanence.

Waahila Rain then went to the pond of Kanawai and

dived under, the water god causing a passage to open underground to the spot indicated, and swam through the water underground till he came out at the place now known as the Punahou Spring. The force of the rushing waters as they burst through the ground soon sufficed to make a small basin, which the boy proceeded to bank and wall up, leaving a narrow outlet for the surplus waters. With the invisible help of the old water god, he immediately set to work to excavate a good-sized pond for his sister to swim in, and when she awoke from a noonday nap, she was astonished to behold a lovely sheet of water where, in the morning, was only dry land. Her brother was swimming and splashing about in it, and gayly called to his sister to come and try her bathing-place.

Kauawaahila afterward made some kalo patches, and people, attracted by the water and consequent fertility of the place, came and settled about, voluntarily offering themselves as vassals to the twins. More and more kalo patches were excavated, and the place became a thriving settlement. The spring became known as *Ka Punahou* (the new spring), and gave its name to the surrounding place.

About this time Kahaakea returned, and hearing of the persecutions to which his beloved children had been subjected, killed Hawea and then himself. Rocky Hill, the home of the children, was called after him, and is known by that name to the present day. Hawea has ever since then been a synonym in the Hawaiian mind for a cruel stepmother.

The Mountain Mist and Waahila Rain afterward

returned to the home of their infancy, Kaala, where they would stay a while, occasionally visiting Konahuanui and upper Manoa Valley, and may be met with in these places at the present day.

They also occasionally visited Punahou, which was under their especial care and protection; but when the land and spring passed into the hands of foreigners, who did not pay homage to the twins, and who allowed the springs to be defiled by the washing of unclean articles and by the bathing of unclean persons, the twins indignantly left the place, and retired to the head of Manoa Valley.

They sometimes pass swiftly over their old home on their way to Kaala, or Konahuanui, and on such occasions will sometimes linger sorrowfully for a few minutes about Rocky Hill. The rain-water pond of Kanawai is now always dry, as the shrubs and bushes which supplied the food of the twins favored of the gods have disappeared. Old natives say that there is now no inducement for the gentle rain of the Uakiowao and Uawaahila to visit those bare hills and plains, as they would find no food there.

XIII

OAHUNUI

MRS. E. M. NAKUINA

ON the plateau lying between Ewa and Waialua, on the island of Oahu, and about a mile off, and mauka of the Kaukonahua bridge, is the historical place called Kukaniloko. This was the ancient birthplace of the Oahu kings and rulers. It was incumbent on all women of the royal line to retire to this place when about to give birth to a child, on pain of forfeiting the rank, privileges, and prerogatives of her expected offspring, should that event happen in a less sacred place.

The stones were still standing some years ago, and perhaps are yet undisturbed, where the royal accouchements took place. In ancient times this locality was taboo ground, for here the high priest of the island had his headquarters. Himself descended from the chief families, and being, in many instances, an uncle or younger brother of the reigning king, or connected by marriage with those of the royal line, and being also at the head of a numerous, well organized, and powerful priesthood, his influence was hardly second to that of the king, and in some matters his authority was paramount.

A few miles mauka of Kukaniloko, toward the Wai-mea Mountains, is Helemano, where the last of the cannibal chiefs from the South Seas finally settled when driven from the plains of Mokuleia and Waialua by the inhabitants of those districts; for the people had been exasperated by the frequent requisitions on the *kamaainas* (original inhabitants) by the stranger chiefs to furnish material for their cannibal feasts.

To the east of Helemano, and about the same dis-tance from Kukaniloko, is Oahunui (Greater Oahu), another historical place. This was the residence of the kings of the island. Tradition has it that previous to the advent of the cannibal strangers the place was known by another name.

When the Lo Aikanaka, as the last of the man-eating chiefs are called, were constrained to take up their residence in upper Helemano, a district just out-side of the boundaries of those reserved for the royal and priestly residences, a young man called Oahunui was king. An elder sister named Kilikiliula, who had been as a mother to him, was supposed to share equally with him the royal power and prerogative. This sister was married to a chief named Lehuanui, of the priestly line, but one not otherwise directly connected with royalty, and was the mother of three children; the two eldest being boys and the youngest a girl. They all lived together in the royal enclosure, but in separate houses, according to ancient custom.

Now, the Lo Aikanaka, on establishing themselves in upper Helemano, had at first behaved very well. They had been circumspect and prudent in their intercourse with the royal retainers, and had visited the young King to render their homage with every appearance of humility.

Oahunui was quite captivated by the plausible, suave manners of the ingratiating southern chief and those of his immediate retainers, and he invited them to a feast.

This civility was reciprocated, and the King dined with the strangers. Here it was strongly suspected that the dish of honor placed before the King was human flesh, served under the guise of pork.

The King found the dish very much to his liking, and intimated to the Lo Aikanaka chief that his *aipuu-puu* (chief cook or steward) understood the preparation and cooking of pork better than the royal cook did.

The Lo Aikanaka took the hint, and the young King became a very frequent guest at the Southerner's board—or rather, mat table. Some excuse or other would be given to invite the royal guest, such as a challenge to the King to a game of *konane* (a game like checkers); or a contest of skill in the different athletic and warlike sports would be arranged, and Oahunui would be asked to be the judge, or simply invited to view them. As a matter of course, it would be expected that the King would remain after the sports and partake of food when on friendly visits of this nature. Thus with one excuse or another he spent a great deal of his time with his new subjects and friends.

To supply the particular dainty craved by the royal visitor, the Lo Aikanaka had to send out warriors to the passes leading to Waianae from Lihue and Kalena, and also to the lonely pathway leading up to Kalakini, on the Waimea side, there to lie in ambush for any lone traveller, or belated person after la-i, aaho, or ferns. Such a one would fall an easy prey to the Lo Aikanaka stalwarts, skilful in the art of the *lua* (to kill by breaking the bones).

This went on for some time, until the unaccountable disappearance of so many people began to be connected with the frequent entertainments by the southern chief. Oahunui's subjects began to hint that their young King had acquired the taste for human flesh at these feasts, and that it was to gratify his unnatural appetite for the horrid dish that he paid his frequent visits to those who were his inferiors, contrary to all royal precedent.

The people's disapproval of the intimacy of Oahunui with his new friends was expressed more and more openly, and the murmurs of discontent grew loud and deep. His chiefs and high priest became alarmed, and begged him to discontinue his visits, or they would not be answerable for the consequences. The King was thereby forced to heed their admonitions and promised to keep away from Lo's, and did so for quite a while.

Now, all the male members of the royal family ate their meals with the King when he was at home. This included, among others, Lehuanui, his sister's husband, and their two sons—healthy, chubby little lads of about eight and six years of age. One day after breakfast, as the roar of the surf at Waialua could be distinctly heard, the King remarked that the fish of Ukoa pond at Waialua must be pressing on to the *makaha* (floodgates) and he would like some aholehole.

This observation really meant a command to his brother-in-law to go and get the fish, as he was the highest chief present except his two royal nephews, too small to assume such duties.

Lehuanui, Kilikiliula's husband, accordingly went to Waialua with a few of his own family retainers and a number of those belonging to the King. They found the fish packed thick at the makaha, and were soon busily engaged in scooping out, cleaning, and salting them. It was quite late at night when Lehuanui, fatigued with the labors of the day, lay down to rest. He had been asleep but a short time when he seemed to see his two sons standing by his head. The eldest spoke to him: "Why do you sleep, my father? While you are down here we are being eaten by your brother-in-law, the King. We were cooked and eaten up, and our skulls are now hanging in a net from a branch of the lehua-tree you are called after, and the rest of our bones are tied in a bundle and buried under the tree by the big root running to the setting sun."

Then they seemed to fade away, and Lehuanui started up, shivering with fear. He hardly knew whether he had been dreaming or had actually seen an apparition of his little sons. He had no doubt they were dead, and as he remembered all the talk and innuendoes about the King's supposed reasons for visiting the strangers and the enforced cessation of those visits at the urgent request of the high priest and the chiefs, he came to the conclusion that the King had expressed a desire for fish in his presence only to send him out of the way. He reasoned that no doubt the King had noticed the chubby forms and rounded limbs of the little lads, and being debarred a chance of partaking surreptitiously of human flesh, had compelled his servants to kill, cook, and serve up his own nephews. In satisfying his depraved appetite, he had also got rid of two who might become formidable rivals; for it was quite within the possibilities that the priests and chiefs in the near future, should he be suspected of a desire for a further indulgence in cannibal diet, might depose him, and proclaim either one of the young nephews his successor.

The father was so troubled that he aroused his immediate body servant, and the two left Waialua for home shortly after midnight. They arrived at the royal enclosure at dawn, and went first to the lehua-tree spoken of by the apparition of the child, and on looking up amid the branches, sure enough there dangled two little skulls in a large-meshed fishing-net. Lehuanui then stooped down and scraped away the leaves and loose dirt from the root indicated, and out rolled a bundle of tapa, which on being opened was found to contain the bones of two children. The father reached up for the net containing the skulls, and putting the bundle of tapa in it, tied the net around his neck. The servant stood by, a silent and grieved spectator of a scene whose meaning he fully understood.

The father procured a stone adze and went to the King's sleeping-house, the servant still following. Here every one but an old woman tending the kukui-nut candle was asleep. Oahunui was stretched out on a pile of soft mats covered with his *paiula*, the royal red kapa of old. The cruel wretch had eaten to excess of the hateful dish he craved, and having accompanied it with copious draughts of awa juice, was in a heavy, drunken sleep.

Lehuanui stood over him, adze in hand, and called, " O King, where are my children?" The stupefied King only stirred uneasily, and would not, or could not, awake. Lehuanui called him three times, and the sight of the drunken brute, gorged with his flesh and blood, so enraged the father that he struck at Oahunui's neck with his stone adze, and severed the head from the body at one blow.

The father and husband then strode to his own sleeping-house, where his wife lay asleep with their youngest child in her arms. He aroused her and asked for his boys. The mother could only weep, without answering. He upbraided her for her devotion to her brother, and for having tamely surrendered her children to satisfy the appetite of the inhuman monster. He reminded her that she had equal power with her brother, and that the latter was very unpopular, and had she chosen to resist his demands and called on the retainers to defend her children, the King would have been killed and her children saved.

He then informed her that, as she had given up his children to be killed for her brother, he had killed him in retaliation, and, saying, "You have preferred your brother to me and mine, so you will see no more of me and mine," he tore the sleeping child from her arms and turned to leave the house.

The poor wife and mother followed, and, flinging herself on her husband, attempted to detain him by clinging to his knees; but the father, crazed by his loss and the thought of her greater affection for a cruel, inhuman brother than for her own children, struck at her with all his might, exclaiming, "Well, then, follow your brother," and rushed away, followed by all his retainers.

Kilikiliula fell on the side of the stream opposite to where the lehua-tree stood, and is said to have turned to stone. The stone is pointed out to this day, balanced on the hillside of the ravine formed by the stream, and is one of the objects for the Hawaiian sightseer.

The headless body of Oahunui lay where he was killed, abandoned by every one. The story runs that in process of time it also turned to stone, as a witness to the anger of the gods and their detestation of his horrible crime. All the servants who had in any way been concerned, in obedience to royal mandate, in killing and cooking the young princes were, at the death of Kilikiliula, likewise turned to stone, just as they were, in the various positions of crouching, kneeling, or sitting. All the rest of the royal retainers, with the lesser chiefs and guards, fled in fear and disgust from the place, and thus the once sacred royal home of the Oahuan chiefs was abandoned and deserted.

The great god Kane's curse, it is believed, still hangs over the desolate spot, in proof of which it is asserted that, although all this happened hundreds of years ago, no one has ever lived there since.

XIV

AHUULA

A LEGEND OF KANIKANIAULA AND THE FIRST FEATHER CLOAK

MRS. E. M. NAKUINA

ELEIO was a *kukini* (trained runner) in the service of Kakaalaneo, King of Maui, several runners being always kept by each king or *alii* of consequence. These kukinis, when sent on any errand, always took a direct line for their destination, climbing hills with the agility of goats, jumping over rocks and streams, and leaping from precipices. They were so fleet of foot that the common illustration of the fact among the natives was the saying that when a kukini was sent on an errand that would ordinarily take a day and a night, fish wrapped in ki leaves (known as *lawalu*), if put on the fire on his starting, would not be cooked sufficiently to be turned before he would be back. Being so serviceable to the aliis, kukinis always enjoyed a high degree of consideration, freedom, and immunity from the strict etiquette and unwritten laws of a Hawaiian court. There was hardly anything so valuable in their master's possession that they could not have it if they wished.

Eleio was sent to Hana to fetch awa for the King,

and was expected to be back in time for the King's supper.   Kakaalaneo was then living at Lahaina. Now, Eleio was not only a kukini, but he was also a kahuna, and had been initiated in the ceremonies and observances by which he was enabled to see spirits or wraiths, and was skilled in medicines, charms, etc., and could return a wandering spirit to its body unless decomposition had set in.

Soon after leaving Olowalu, and as he commenced the ascent of Aalaloloa, he saw a beautiful young woman ahead of him.   He naturally hastened his steps, intending to overtake such a charming fellow-traveller; but, do what he would, she kept always just so far ahead of him.   Being the fleetest and most renowned kukini of his time, it roused his professional pride to be outrun by a woman, even if only for a short distance ; so he was determined to catch her, and he gave himself entirely to that effort.   The young woman led him a weary chase over rocks, hills, mountains, deep ravines, precipices, and dark streams, till they came to the *Lae* (cape) of Hanamanuloa at Kahikinui, beyond Kaupo, when he caught her just at the entrance to a *puoa*.   A puoa was a kind of tower, generally of bamboo, with a platform half-way up, on which the dead bodies of persons of distinction belonging to certain families or classes were exposed to the elements.

When Eleio caught the young woman she turned to him and cried: "Let me live! I am not human, but a spirit, and inside this inclosure is my dwelling."

He answered: "I have been aware for some time

of your being a spirit. No human being could have so outrun me."

She then said: "Let us be friends. In yonder house live my parents and relatives. Go to them and ask for a hog, kapas, some fine mats, and a feather cloak. Describe me to them and tell them that I give all those things to you. The feather cloak is unfinished. It is now only a fathom and a half square, and was intended to be two fathoms. There are enough feathers and netting in the house to finish it. Tell them to finish it for you." The spirit then disappeared.

Eleio entered the puoa, climbed on to the platform, and saw the dead body of the girl. She was in every way as beautiful as the spirit had appeared to him, and apparently decomposition had not yet set in. He left the puoa and hurried to the house pointed out by the spirit as that of her friends, and saw a woman wailing, whom, from the resemblance, he at once knew to be the mother of the girl; so he saluted her with an aloha. He then said: "I am a stranger here, but I had a travelling companion who guided me to yonder puoa and then disappeared." At these strange words the woman stopped wailing and called to her husband, to whom she repeated what the stranger had said. The latter then asked: "Does this house belong to you?"

Husband and wife, wondering, answered at once: "It does."

"Then," said Eleio, "my message is to you. My travelling companion has a hog a fathom in length in your care; also a pile of fine kapas of Paiula and others of fine quality; also a pile of mats and an unfinished feather cloak, now a fathom and a half in length, which you are to finish, the materials being in the house. All these things she has given to me, and sent me to you for them." Then he began to describe the young woman. Both parents recognized the truthfulness of the description, and willingly agreed to give up the things which their beloved daughter must have herself given away. But when they spoke of killing the hog and making an *ahaaina* (feast) for him, whom they had immediately resolved to adopt as a son, he said: "Wait a little and let me ask: Are all these people I see around this place your friends?"

They both answered: "They are our relatives— uncles, aunts, and cousins to the spirit, who seems to have adopted you either as husband or brother."

"Will they do your bidding in everything?" he asked.

They answered that they could be relied upon. He directed them to build a large *lanai*, or arbor, to be entirely covered with ferns, ginger, maile, and ieie — the sweet and odorous foliage greens of the islands. An altar was to be erected at one end of the lanai and appropriately decorated. The order was willingly carried out, men, women, and children working with a will, so that the whole structure was finished in a couple of hours.

Eleio now directed the hog to be cooked. He also ordered cooked red and white fish, red, white, and black cocks, and bananas of the lele and maoli varie-

ties, to be placed on the altar. He ordered all women
and children to enter their houses and to assist him
with their prayers; all pigs, chickens, and dogs to be
tied in dark huts to keep them quiet, and that the
most profound silence should be kept. The men at
work were asked to remember their gods, and to
invoke their assistance for Eleio. He then started for
Hana, pulled up a couple of bushes of awa of Kaeleku,
famous for its medicinal properties, and was back again
before the hog was cooked. The awa was prepared,
and when the preparations for the feast were complete
and set out, he offered everything to his gods and
begged assistance in what he was about to perform.

It seems the spirit of the girl had been lingering
near him all the time, seeming to be attached to him,
but of course invisible to every one. When Eleio
had finished his invocation he turned and caught the
spirit, and, holding his breath and invoking the gods,
he hurried to the puoa, followed by the parents, who
now began to understand that he was going to try the
kapuku (or restoration to life of the dead) on their
daughter. Arriving at the puoa, he placed the spirit
against the insteps of the girl and pressed it firmly in,
meanwhile continuing his invocation. The spirit
entered its former tenement kindly enough until it
came to the knees, when it refused to go any further,
as from there it could perceive that the stomach was
beginning to decompose, and it did not want to be
exposed to the pollution of decaying matter. But
Eleio, by the strength of his prayers, was enabled to
push the spirit up past the knees till it came to the

thigh bones, when the refractory spirit again refused to proceed. He had to put additional fervor into his prayers to overcome the spirit's resistance, and it proceeded up to the throat, when there was some further check; by this time the father, mother, and male relatives were all grouped around anxiously watching the operation, and they all added the strength of their petitions to those of Eleio, which enabled him to push the spirit past the neck, when the girl gave a sort of crow. There was now every hope of success, and all the company renewed their prayers with redoubled vigor. The spirit made a last feeble resistance at the elbows and wrists, which was triumphantly overborne by the strength of the united prayers. Then it quietly submitted, took complete possession of the body, and the girl came to life. She was submitted to the usual ceremonies of purification by the local priest, after which she was led to the prepared lanai, when kahuna, maid, parents, and relatives had a joyous reunion. Then they feasted on the food prepared for the gods, who were only supposed to absorb the spiritual essence of things, leaving the grosser material parts to their devotees, who, for the time being, are considered their guests.

After the feast the feather cloak, kapas, and fine mats were brought and displayed to Eleio; and the father said to him: "Take the woman thou hast restored and have her for wife, and remain here with us; you will be our son and will share equally in the love we have for her."

But our hero, with great self-denial and fidelity,

said: "No, I accept her as a charge, but for wife, she is worthy to be one for a higher than I. If you will trust her to me, I will take her to my master, for by her beauty and charms she is worthy to be the queen of our lovely island."

The father answered: "She is yours to do with as you will. It is as if you had created her, for without you, where would she be now? We only ask this, that you always remember that you have parents and relatives here, and a home whenever you choose."

Eleio then asked that the feather cloak be finished for him before he returned to his master. All who could work at feathers set about it at once, including the fair girl restored to life; and he now learned that she was called Kanikaniaula.

When it was completed he set out on his return to Lahaina accompanied by the girl, and taking the feather cloak and the remaining awa he had not used in his incantations. They travelled slowly according to the strength of Kanikaniaula, who now in the body could not equal the speed she had displayed as a spirit.

Arriving at Launiupoko, Eleio turned to her and said: "You wait and hide here in the bushes while I go on alone. If by sundown I do not return, I shall be dead. You know the road by which we came; then return to your people. But if all goes well with me I shall be back in a little while."

He then went on alone, and when he reached Makila, on the confines of Lahaina, he saw a number of people heating an *imu*, or underground oven. On perceiving him they started to bind and roast him alive, such being the orders of the King, but he ordered them away with the request, "Let me die at the feet of my master." And thus he passed successfully the imu heated for him.

When he finally stood before Kakaalaneo, the latter said to him: "How is this? Why are you not cooked alive, as I ordered? How came you to pass my lunas?"

The kukini answered: "It was the wish of the slave to die at the feet of his master, if die he must; but if so, it would be an irreparable loss to you, my master, for I have that with me that will cause your name to be renowned and handed down to posterity."

"And what is that?" questioned the King.

Eleio then unrolled his bundle and displayed to the astonished gaze of the King and courtiers the glories of a feather cloak, before then unheard of on the islands. Needless to say, he was immediately pardoned and restored to royal favor, and the awa he had brought from Hana was reserved for the King's special use in his offerings to the gods that evening.

When the King heard the whole story of Eleio's absence, and that the fair original owner was but a short way off, he ordered her to be immediately brought before him that he might express his gratitude for the wonderful garment. When she arrived, he was so struck with her beauty and modest deportment that he asked her to become his Queen. Thus, some of the highest chiefs of the land traced their descent from Kakaalaneo and Kanikaniaula.

The original feather cloak, known as the "*Ahu o Kakaalaneo*," is said to be in the possession of the Pauahi Bishop Museum. At one time it was used on state occasions as a *pa-u*, or skirt, by Princess Nahienaena, own sister of the second and third Kamehamehas.

The ahuulas of the ancient Hawaiians were of fine netting, entirely covered with feathers, woven in. These were either of one color and kind or two or three different colors outlining patterns. The feathers were knotted by twos or threes with twisted strands of the olona, the process being called *uo*. They were then woven into the foundation netting previously made the exact shape and size wanted. The whole process of feather cloak making was laborious and intricate, and the making of a cloak took a great many years. And as to durability, let the cloak of Kalaalaneo, now several centuries old, attest.

XV

KAALA AND KAAIALII

A LEGEND OF LANAI

W. M. GIBSON

BORDERING upon the land of Kealia, on the southwest coast of Lanai, where was a *pahonua*, or place of refuge, are the remains of Kaunolu, an ancient *heiau*, or temple. Its ruins lie within the mouth of a deep ravine, whose extending banks run out into the sea and form a bold, bluff-bound bay. On the top of the western bank there is a stone-paved platform, called the *kuaha*. Outside of this, and separated by a narrow alley-way, there runs a broad high wall, which quite encircles the kuaha. Other walls and structures lead down the bank, and the slope is terraced and paved down to the tide-worn stones of the shore.

At the beach there is a break; a great block of the bluff has been rent away by some convulsion of nature, and stands out like a lone tower, divided from the main by a gulf of the sea. Its high walls beetle from their tops, upon which neither man nor goat can climb. But you can behold on the flat summit of this islet bluff, portions of ancient work, of altars and walls, and no doubt part of the mainland temple, to which this fragment once was joined. But man can visit this lone tower's top no more, and his feet can never climb its overhanging walls.

Inland from the temple there are many remains of the huts of the people of the past. The stone foundations, the inclosures for swine, the round earth ovens, and other traces of a throng of people cover many acres of beach and hillside. This was a town famed as an abode of gods and a refuge for those who fled for their lives; but it drew its people mainly through the fame of its fishing-ground, which swarmed with the varied life of the Hawaiian seas.

To this famed fishing-ground came the great hero of Hawaii to tax the deep, when he had subdued this and the other isles. He came with his fleets of war canoes; with his faithful *koas*, or fighting men, with his chiefs, and priests, and women, and their trains. He had a house here. Upon the craggy bluff that forms the eastern bank of the bay there is a lonely *pa*, or wall, and stones of an ancient fort, overlooking the temple, town, and bay.

Kamehameha came to Kealia for sport rather than for worship. Who so loved to throw the maika ball, or hurl the spear, or thrust aside the many javelins flung at his naked chest, as the chief of Kohala? He rode gladly on the crest of the surf waves. He delighted to drive his canoe alone out into the storm. He fought with the monsters of the deep, as well as with men. He captured the great shark that abounds in the bay, and he would clutch in the fearful grip of his hands the deadly eel or snake of these seas, the terror of fishes and men.

When this warrior king came to Kaunolu, the islanders thronged to the shore to pay homage to the great chief, and to lay at the feet of their sovereign, as was their wont, the products of the isle: the taro, the yam, the hala, the cocoanut, ohelo, banana, and sweet potato. They piled up a mound of food before the door of the King's pakui, along with a clamorous multitude of fat poi-fed dogs, and of fathom-long swine.

Besides this tribute of the men, the workers of the land, the women filled the air with the sweet odors of their floral offerings. The maidens were twined from head to waist with *leis* or wreaths of the *na-u*, which is Lanai's own lovely jessamine—a rare gardenia, whose sweet aroma loads the breeze, and leads you to the bush when seeking it afar off. These garlands were fastened to the plaited pili thatch of the King's pakui; they were placed on the necks of the young warriors, who stood around the chief; and around his royal brows they twined an odorous crown of maile.

The brightest of the girlish throng who stood before the dread Lord of the Isles was Kaala, or Sweet Scented, whose fifteen suns had just burnished her sweet brown face with a soft golden gloss; and her large, round, tender eyes knew yet no wilting fires. Her neck and arms, and all of her young body not covered by the leafy pa-u, was tinted with a soft sheen like unto a rising moon. Her skin glowed with the glory of youth, and mingled its delicate odor of health with the blooms of the groves, so that the perfume of her presence received fittingly the name of Fragrance.

In those rude days the island race was sound and clean. The supple round limbs were made bright and strong by the constant bath and the temperate breeze. They were not cumbered with clothing; they wore no long, sweating gowns, but their smooth, shining skins reflected back their sun, which gave them such a rich and dusky charm.

Perhaps such a race cannot long wear all our gear and live. They are best clothed with sea foam, or with the garlands of their groves. How sweetly blend the brown and green; and when young, soft, amber-tinted cheeks, glowing with the crimson tide beneath, are wreathed with the odorous evergreens of the isles, you see the poesy of our kind, and the sweet, wild grace that dwelt in the Eden Paradise.

The sweet Kaala stood mindless of harm, as the playful breeze rustled the long blades of the la-i (*dracæna*) leaves, hanging like a bundle of green swords from her waist; and as they twirled and fluttered in the air, revealed the soft, rounded form, whose charm filled the eye and heart of one who stood among the braves of the great chief—the heart of the stout young warrior Kaaialii.

This youth had fought in the battle of Maunalei, Lanai's last bloody fight. With his long-reaching spear, wielded with sinewy arms, he urged the flying foe to the top of a fearful cliff, and mocking the cries of a huddled crowd of panic-scared men, drove them with thrusts and shouts till they leaped like frightened sheep into the jaws of the deep, dark chasm, and their torn corses strewed the jagged stones below.

Kaaialii, like many a butcher of his kind, was comely to see. With the lion's heart, he had the lion's tawny hue. A swart grace beamed beneath his curling brows. He had the small, firm hand to throttle or caress, and eyes full of fire for hate or love; and love's flame now lit the face of the hero of the bloody leap, and to his great chief he said, "O King of all the isles, let this sweet flower be mine, rather than the valley thou gavest me for my domain."

Said Kamehameha: "You shall plant the Lanai jessamine in the valley I gave you in Kohala. But there is another who claims our daughter, who is the stout bone-breaker, the scarred Mailou. My spearman of Maunalei can have no fear; and you shall wrestle with him; and let the one whose arms can clasp the girl after the fight carry her to his house, where one kapa shall cover the two."

The poor maid, the careless gift of savage power, held up her clasped hands with a frightened gesture at the dread name of the breaker of bones; for she had heard how he had sucked the breath of many a dainty bloom like her, then crunched the wilted blossom with sinews of hate, and flung it to the sharks.

And the Lanai maiden loved the young chief of Hawaii. He had indeed pierced her people, but only the tender darts of his eyes had wounded her. Turning to him, she looked her savage, quick, young love, and said, "O Kaaialii, may thy grip be as sure as thy thrust. Save me from the bloody virgin-eater, and I will catch the squid and beat the kapa for thee all my days."

The time of contest approached. The King sat under the shade of a leafy *kou*, the royal tree of the olden time, which has faded away with the chiefs it once did shelter. On the smooth shell floor, covered with the hala mat, stood the bare-limbed braves, stripped to the malo, who with hot eyes of hate shot out their rage of lust and blood, and stretched out their strangling arms. They stood, beating with heavy fists their broad, glossy chests of bronze, and grinning face to face, they glowered their savage wish to kill. Then, with right foot advanced, and right arm uplifted, they pause to shout their gage of battle, and tell to each how they would maim and tear, and kill, and give each other's flesh for food to some beastly maw.

And now, each drawing near to each, with arms uplifted, and outspread palms with sinewy play, like nervy claws trying to clutch or grip, they seek a chance for a deadly clinch. And swift the scarred child-strangler has sprung with his right to the young spear-man's throat, who as quickly hooks the lunging arm within the crook of his, and with quick, sledge-like blow breaks the shoulder arm-bone.

With fury the baffled bone-breaker grips with the uncrippled hand; but now two stout young arms, tense with rage, soon twist and break the one unaided limb. Then with limp arms the beaten brute turns to flee; but swift hate is upon him, and clutches him by the throat; and pressing him down, the hero of Kaala holds his knee to the hapless wretch's back, and with knee bored into the backward bended spine, he strains

and jerks till the jointed bones snap and break, and
the dread throttler of girls and babes lies prone on the
mat, a broken and bloody corse.

"Good!" cried the King. "Our son has the strength
of Kanekoa.   Now let our daughter soothe the limbs
of her lover.   Let her stroke his skin, press his joints,
and knead his back with the loving grip and touch of
the lomilomi.   We will have a great bake, with the
hula and song; and when the feast is over, then shall
they be one."

A line of women squat down. They crone their
wild refrain, praising the one who wins in strife and
love. They seize in their right hand the hula gourd,
clattering with pebbles inside. They whirl it aloft,
they shake, they swing, they strike their palms, they
thump the mat; and now with supple joints they twirl
their loins, and with heave and twist, and with swing
and song, the savage dance goes on.

Kaala stood up with the maiden throng, the tender,
guarded gifts of kings. They twined their wreaths,
they swayed, and posed their shining arms; and flap-
ping with their hands their leafy skirts, revealed their
rounded limbs. This fires the gaze of men, and the
hero of the day with flaming eyes, springs and clasps
his love, crying as he bears her away: "Thou shalt
dance in my hut in Kohala for me alone, forever!"

At this, a stout yet grizzled man of the isle lifts up
his voice and wails: "Kaala, my child, is gone. Who
shall soothe my limbs when I return from spearing
the ohua? And who shall feed me with taro and
bread-fruit like the chief of Olowalu, when I have no

daughter to give away? I must hide from the chief or I die." And thus wailed out Opunui, the father of Kaala.

But a fierce hate stirred the heart of Opunui. His friend was driven over the cliff at Maunalei, and he himself had lived only by crawling at the feet of the slayer. He hid his hate, and planned to save his girl and balk the killer of his people. He said in his heart, "I will hide her in the sea, and none but the fish gods and I shall know where the ever-sounding surf surges over Kaala."

Now, in the morn, when the girl with ruddy brown cheeks, and glowing with the brightening dawn of love, stood in the doorway of the lodge of her lord, and her face was sparkling with the sheen from the sun, her sire in humble guise stood forth and said, "My child, your mother at Mahana is dying. Pray you, my lord, your love, that you may see her once more before his canoe shall bear you to his great land."

"Alas!" said the tender child, "since when is Kalani ill? I shall carry to her this large sweet fish speared by my lord; and when I have rubbed her aching limbs, she will be well again with the love touch of her child. Yes, my lord will let me go. Will you not, O Kaaialii; will you not let me go to give my mother a last embrace, and I shall be back again before the moon has twice spanned the bay?"

The hero clasped his young love with one stout twining arm, and gazing into her eyes, he with a caressing hand put back from her brow her shining hair, and thus to his heart's life he spoke: "O my sweet flower, how shall I live without thee, even for this day's march of the sun? For thou art my very breath, and I shall pant and die like a stranded fish without thee. But no, let me not say so. Kaaialii is a chief who has fought men and sharks; and he must not speak like a girl. He too loves his mother, who looks for him in the valley of Kohala; and shall he deny thy mother, to look her last upon the sweet face and the tender limbs that she fed and reared for him? Go, my Kaala. But thy chief will sit and watch with a hungering heart, till thou come back to his arms again."

And the pretty jessamine twined her arms around his neck, and laying her cheek upon his breast said, with upturned tender glances, "O my chief, who gavest me life and sweet joy; thy breath is my breath; thy eyes are my sweetest sight; thy breast is my only resting-place; and when I go away, I shall all the way look back to thee, and go slowly with a backward turned heart; but when I return to thee, I shall have wings to bear me to my lord."

"Yes, my own bird," said Kaaialii, "thou must fly, but fly swiftly in thy going as well as in thy coming; for both ways thou fliest to me. When thou art gone I shall spear the tender ohua fish, I shall bake the yam and banana, and I will fill the calabash with sweet water, to feed thee, my heart, when thou shalt come; and thou shalt feed me with thy loving eyes.

"Here, Opunui! take thy child. Thou gavest life to her, but now she gives life to me. Bring her back all well, ere the sun has twice risen. If she come not soon, I shall die; but I should slay thee before I die; therefore, O Opunui, hasten thy going and thy coming, and bring back my life and love to me."

And now the stern hero unclasped the weeping girl. His eye was calm, but his shut lips showed the work within of a strong and tender heart of love. He felt the ache of a larger woe than this short parting. He pressed the little head between his palms; he kissed the sobbing lips again and again; he gave one strong clasp, heart to heart, and then quickly strode away.

As Kaala tripped along the stony up-hill path, she glanced backward on her way, to get glimpses of him she loved, and she beheld her chief standing on the topmost rock of the great bluff overhanging the sea. And still as she went and looked, still there he stood; and when on the top of the ridge and about to descend into the great valley, she turned to look her last, still she saw her loving lord looking up to her.

The silent sire and the weeping child soon trod the round, green vale of Palawai. She heeded not now to pluck, as was her wont, the flowers in her path; but thought how she should stop a while, as she came back, to twine a wreath for her dear lord's neck. And thus this sad young love tripped along with innocent hope by the moody Opunui's side.

They passed through the groves of Kalulu and Kumoku, and then the man swerved from the path leading to Mahana and turned his face again seaward. At this the sad and silent child looked up into the face of her grim and sullen sire and said: "O father, we shall not find mother on this path, but we shall lose our way and come to the sea once more."

"And thy mother is by the sea, by the bay of Kaumalapau. There she gathers limpets on the rocks. She has dried a large squid for thee. She has pounded some taro and filled her calabash with poi, and would feed thee once more. She is not sick; but had I said she was well, thy lord would not have let thee go; but now thou art on the way to sleep with thy mother by the sea."

The poor weary girl now trudged on with a doubting heart. She glanced sadly at her dread sire's moody eye. Silent and sore she trod the stony path leading down to the shore, and when she came to the beach with naught in view but the rocks and sea, she said with a bursting heart, "O my father, is the shark to be my mother, and I to never see my dear chief any more?"

"Hear the truth," cried Opunui. "Thy home for a time is indeed in the sea, and the shark shall be thy mate, but he shall not harm thee. Thou goest down where the sea god lives, and he shall tell thee that the accursed chief of the bloody leap shall not carry away any daughter of Lanai. When Kaaialii has sailed for Kohala then shall the chief of Olowalu come and bring thee to earth again."

As the fierce sire spoke, he seized the hand of Kaala, and unheeding her sobs and cries, led her along the rugged shore to a point eastward of the bay, where the beating sea makes the rocky shore tremble beneath the feet. Here was a boiling gulf, a fret and foam of

the sea, a roar of waters, and a mighty jet of brine and
spray from a spouting cave whose mouth lay deep
beneath the battling tide.

See yon advancing billow! The south wind sends it
surging along. It rears its combing, whitening crest,
and with mighty, swift-rushing volume of angry green
sea, it strikes the mouth of the cave; it drives and
packs the pent-up air within, and now the tightened
wind rebounds, and driving back the ramming sea,
bursts forth with a roar as the huge spout of sea leaps
upward to the sky, and then comes curving down in
gentle silver spray.

The fearful child now clasped the knees of her savage sire. "Not there, O father," she sobbed and
wailed. "The sea snake (the *puhi*) has his home in
the cave, and he will bite and tear me, and ere I die,
the crawling crabs will creep over me and pick out my
weeping eyes. Alas, O father, better give me to the
shark, and then my cry and moan will not hurt thine
ear."

Opunui clasped the slender girl with one sinewy
arm, and with a bound he leaped into the frothed and
fretted pool below. Downward with a dolphin's ease
he moved, and with his free arm beating back the
brine, moved along the ocean bed into the sea cave's
jagged jaws; and then stemming with stiffened sinew
the wind-driven tide, he swam onward till he struck a
sunless beach and then stood inside the cave, whose
mouth is beneath the sea.

Here was a broad, dry space with a lofty, salt-icicled
roof. The green, translucent sea, as it rolled back and

forth at their feet, gave to their brown faces a ghastly white glare. The scavenger crabs scrambled away over the dank and dripping stones, and the loathsome biting eel, slowly reached out its well-toothed, wide-gaping jaw to tear the tender feet that roused it from its horrid lair, where the dread sea god dwelt.

The poor hapless girl sank down upon this gloomy shore and cried, clinging to the kanaka's knee: "O father, beat out my brains with this jagged stone, and do not let the eel twine around my neck, and trail with a loathsome, slimy, creeping crawl over my body before I die. Oh! the crabs will pick and tear me before my breath is gone."

"Listen," said Opunui. "Thou shalt go back with me to the warm sunny air. Thou shalt tread again the sweet-smelling flowery vale of Palawai, and twine thy neck with wreaths of scented jessamine, if thou wilt go with me to the house of the chief of Olowalu and there let thy bloody lord behold thee wanton with thy love in another chief's arms."

"Never," shouted the lover of Kaaialii, "never will I meet any clasp of love but that of my own chief. If I cannot lay my head again upon his breast, I will lay it in death upon these cold stones. If his arm shall never again draw me to his heart, then let the eel twine my neck and let him tear away my cheeks rather than that another beside my dear lord shall press my face."

"Then let the eel be thy mate," cried Opunui, as he roughly unclasped the tender arms twined around his knees; "until the chief of Olowalu comes to seize thee, and carry thee to his house in the hills of Maui. Seek not to leave the cave. Thou knowest that with thy weak arms, thou wilt tear thyself against the jagged rocks in trying to swim through the swift flowing channel. Stay till I send for thee, and live." Then dashing out into the foaming gulf with mighty buffeting arms he soon reached the upper air.

And Kaaialii stood upon the bluff, looking up to the hillside path by which his love had gone, long after her form was lost to view in the interior vales. And after slight sleep upon his mat, and walking by the shore that night, he came at dawn and climbed the bluff again to watch his love come down the hill. And as he gazed he saw a leafy skirt flutter in the wind, and his heart fluttered to clasp his little girl; but as a curly brow drew near, his soul sank to see it was not his love, but her friend Ua (rain) with some sad news upon her face.

With hot haste and eager asking eyes does the love-lorn chief meet the maiden messenger, and cries, "Why does Kaala delay in the valley? Has she twined wreaths for another's neck for me to break? Has a wild hog torn her? Or has the anaana prayer of death struck her heart, and does she lie cold on the sod of Mahana? Speak quickly, for thy face kills me, O Ua!"

"Not thus, my lord," said the weeping girl, as the soft shower fell from Ua's sweet eyes. "Thy love is not in the valley; and she has not reached the hut of her mother Kalani. But kanakas saw from the hills of Kalulu her father lead her through the forest of

Kumoku; since then our Kaala has not been seen,
and I fear has met some fate, that is to thwart thy
love."

"Kaala lost? The blood of my heart is gone!"
He hears no more! The fierce chief, hot with baffled
passion, strikes madly at the air, and dashes away,
onward up the stony hill; and upward with his stout
young savage thews, he bounds along without halt or
slack of speed till he reaches the valley's rim, then
rushes down its slopes.

He courses over its bright green plains. He sees
in the dusty path some prints that must be those of
the dear feet he follows now. His heart feels a fresh
bound; he feels neither strain of limb nor scantness
of breath, and, searching as he runs, he descries before
him in the plain the deceitful sire alone.

"Opunui," he cries, "give me Kaala, or thy life!"
The stout, gray kanaka looks to see the face of flame
and the outstretched arms, and stops not to try the
strength of his own limbs, or to stay for any parley,
but flies across the valley, along the very path by which
the fierce lover came; and with fear to spur him on,
he keeps well before his well blown foe.

But Kaaialii is now a god; he runs with new strung
limbs, and presses hard this fresh-footed runner of
many a race. They are within two spears' length of
each other's grip upon the rim of the vale; and hot
with haste the one, and with fear the other, they dash
along the rugged path of Kealia, and rush downward
to the sea. They bound o'er the fearful path of
clinkers. Their torn feet heed not the pointed stones.

The elder seeks the shelter of the taboo; and now, both roused by the outcries of a crowd that swarm on the bluffs around, they put forth their remaining strength and strive who shall gain first the entrance to the sacred wall of refuge.

For this the hunted sire strains his fast failing nerve; and the youth with a shout quickens his still tense limbs. He is within a spear's length; he stretches out his arms. Ha, old man! he has thy throat within his grip. But no, the greased neck slips the grasp; the wretch leaps for his dear life, he gains the sacred wall, he bounds inside, and the furious foe is stopped by the staves of priests.

The baffled chief lies prone in the dust, and curses the gods and the sacred taboo. After a time he is led away to his hut by friends; and then the soothing hands of Ua rub and knead the soreness out of his limbs. And when she has set the calabash of poi before him along with the relishing dry squid, and he has filled himself and is strong again, he will not heed any entreaty of chief or friends; not even the caressing lures of Ua, who loves him; but he says, "I will go and seek Kaala; and if I find her not, I die."

Again the love-lorn chief seeks the inland. He shouts the name of his lost love in the groves of Kumoku, and throughout the forest of Mahana. Then he roams through the cloud-canopied valley of Palawai; he searches among the wooded canyons of Kalulu, and he wakes the echoes with the name of Kaala in the gorge of the great ravine of Maunalei. He follows this high walled barranca over its richly flowered and shaded floor; and also along by the winding stream, until he reaches its source, an abrupt wall of stone, one hundred feet high, and forming the head of the ravine. From the face of this steep, towering rock, there exudes a sweet, clear rain, a thousand trickling rills of rock-filtered water leaping from points of fern and moss, and filling up an ice cold pool below, at which our weary chief gladly slaked his thirst. The hero now clambers the steep walls of the gorge, impassable to the steps of men in these days; but he climbs with toes thrust in crannies, or resting on short juts and points of rock; and he pulls himself upward by grasping at out-cropping bushes and strong tufts of fern. And thus with stout sinew and bold nerve the fearless spearman reaches the upper land from whence he had, in his day of devouring rage, hurled and driven headlong the panic-stricken foe.

And now he runs on over the lands of Paomai, through the wooded dells of the gorge of Kaiholena, and onward across Kaunolu and Kalulu, until he reaches the head spring of sacred Kealia called Waiakekua; and here he gathered bananas and ohelo berries; and as he stayed his hunger with the pleasant wild fruit, he beheld a white-haired priest of Kaunolu, bearing a calabash of water.

The aged priest feared the stalwart chief, because he was not upon his own sacred ground, under the safe wing of the taboo; and therefore he bowed low and clasped the stout knees, and offered the water to slake the thirst of the sorrowing chief. But Kaaialii cried out: "I thirst not for water, but for the sight of my love. Tell me where she is hid, and I will bring thee hogs and men for the gods." And to this the glad priest replied:

"Son of the stout spear! I know thou seekest the sweet Flower of Palawai; and no man but her sire has seen her resting-place; but I know that thou seekest in vain in the groves, and in the ravines, and in this mountain. Opunui is a great diver and has his dens in the sea. He leaves the shore when no one follows, and he sleeps with the fish gods, and thou wilt find thy love in some cave of the rock-bound southern shore."

The chief quickly turns his face again seaward. He descends the deep shaded pathway of the ravine of Kaunolu. He winds his way through shaded thickets of ohia, sandalwood, the yellow mamani, the shrub violet, and the fragrant na-u. He halted not as he reached the plain of Palawai, though the ever overhanging canopy of cloud that shades this valley of the mountain cooled his weary feet. These upper lands were still, and no voice was heard by the pili grass huts, and the maika balls and the wickets of the bowling alley of Palawai stood untouched, because all the people were with the great chief by the shore of Kaunolu; and Kaaialii thought that he trod the flowery pathway of the still valley alone.

But there was one who, in soothing his strained limbs after he fell by the gateway of the temple, had planted strong love in her own heart; and she, Ua, with her lithe young limbs, had followed this sorrowing lord through all his weary tramp, even through the gorges, and over the ramparts of the hills, and she was near the sad, wayworn chief when he reached the southern shore.

The weary hero only stayed his steps when he reached the brow of the great bluff of Palikaholo. The sea broke many hundred feet below where he stood. The gulls and screaming boatswain birds sailed in mid-air between his perch and the green waves. He looked up the coast to his right, and saw the lofty, wondrous sea columns of Honopu. He looked to the left, and beheld the crags of Kalulu, but nowhere could he see any sign which should tell him where his love was hid away.

His strong, wild nature was touched by the distant sob and moan of the surf. It sang a song for his sad, savage soul. It roused up before his eyes other eyes, and lips, and cheeks, and clasps of tender arms. His own sinewy ones he now stretched out wildly in the mocking air. He groaned, and sobbed, and beat his breast as he cried out, "Kaala! O Kaala! Where art thou? Dost thou sleep with the fish gods, or must I go to join thee in the great shark's maw?"

As the sad hero thought of this dread devourer of many a tender child of the isles, he hid his face with his hands,—looking with self-torture upon the image of his soft young love, crunched, bloody and shrieking, in the jaws of the horrid god of the Hawaiian seas; and as he thought and waked up in his heart the memories of his love, he felt that he must seek her even in her gory grave in the sea.

Then he looks forth again, and as he gazes down

by the shore his eyes rest upon the spray of the blowing cave near Kaumalapau. It leaps high with the
swell which the south wind sends. The white mist
gleams in the sun. Shifting forms and shades are
seen in the varied play of the up-leaping cloud. And
as with fevered soul he glances, he sees a form spring
up in the ever bounding spray.

He sees with his burning eyes the lines of the sweet
form that twines with tender touch around his soul.
He sees the waving hair, that mingles on his neck
with his own swart curls. He sees,—he thinks he
sees,—in the leap and play of sun-tinted spray, his love,
his lost Kaala; and with hot foot he rushes downward
to the shore.

He stands upon the point of rock whence Opunui
sprang. He feels the throb beneath his feet of the
beating, bounding tide. He sees the fret and foam
of the surging gulf below the leaping spray, and is
wetted by the shore-driven mist. He sees all of this
wild, working water, but he does not see Kaala.

And yet he peers into this mad surf for her he
seeks. The form that he has seen still leads him on.
He will brave the sea god's wrath; and he fain would
cool his brow of flame in the briny bath. He thinks
he hears a voice sounding down within his soul; and
cries, "Where art thou, O Kaala? I come, I come!"
And as he cries, he springs into the white, foaming
surge of this ever fretted sea.

And one was near as the hero sprang; even Ua, with
the clustering curls. She loved the chief; she did
hope that when his steps were stayed by the sea, and

he had mingled his moan with the wild waters' wail, that he would turn once more to the inland groves, where she would twine him wreaths, and soothe his limbs, and rest his head upon her knees; but he has leaped for death, he comes up no more. And Ua wailed for Kaaialii; and as the chief rose no more from out the lashed and lathered sea, she cried out, *"Auwe ka make!"* (Alas, he is dead!) And thus wailing and crying out, and tearing her hair, she ran back over the bluffs, and down the shore to the tabooed ground of Kealia, and wailing ever, flung herself at the feet of Kamehameha.

The King was grieved to hear from Ua of the loss of his young chief. But the priest Papalua standing near, said: "O Chief of Heaven, and of all the isles; there where Kaaialii has leaped is the sea den of Opunui, and as thy brave spearman can follow the turtle to his deep sea nest, he will see the mouth of the cave, and in it, I think, he will find his lost love, Kaala, the flower of Palawai."

At this Ua roused up. She called to her brother Keawe, and laying hold on him, pulled him toward the shore, crying out, "To thy canoe, quick! I will help thee to paddle to Kaumalapau." For thus she could reach the cave sooner than by the way of the bluffs. And the great chief also following, sprang into his swiftest canoe, and helping as was his wont, plunged his blade deep into the swelling tide, and bounded along by the frowning shore of Kumoku.

When Kaaialii plunged beneath the surging waters, he became at once the searching diver of the Hawaiian seas; and as his keen eye peered throughout the depths, he saw the portals of the ocean cave into which poured the charging main. He then, stemming with easy play of his well-knit limbs the suck and rush of the sea, shot through the current of the gorge; and soon stood up upon the sunless strand.

At first he saw not, but his ears took in at once a sad and piteous moan,—a sweet, sad moan for his hungry ear, of the voice of her he sought. And there upon the cold, dank, dismal floor he could dimly see his bleeding, dying love. Quickly clasping and soothing her, he lifted her up to bear her to the upper air; but the moans of his poor weak Kaala told him she would be strangled in passing through the sea.

And as he sat down, and held her in his arms, she feebly spoke: "O my chief, I can die now! I feared that the fish gods would take me, and I should never see thee more. The eel bit me, and the crabs crawled over me, and when I dared the sea to go and seek thee, my weak arms could not fight the tide; I was torn against the jaws of the cave, and this and the fear of the gods have so hurt me, that I must die."

"Not so, my love," said the sad and tearful chief. "I am with thee now. I give thee the warmth of my heart. Feel my life in thine. Live, O my Kaala, for me. Come, rest and be calm, and when thou canst hold thy breath I will take thee to the sweet air again, and to thy valley, where thou shalt twine wreaths for me." And thus with fond words and caresses he sought to soothe his love.

But the poor girl still bled as she moaned; and with

fainter voice she said, "No, my chief, I shall never twine a wreath, but only my arms once more around thy neck." And feebly clasping him, she said in sad, sobbing, fainting tones, "Aloha, my sweet lord! Lay me among the flowers by Waiakeakua, and do not slay my father."

Then, breathing moans and murmurs of love, she lay for a time weak and fainting upon her lover's breast, with her arms drooping by her side. But all at once she clasps his neck, and with cheek to cheek, she clings, she moans, she gasps her last throbs of love and passes away; and her poor torn corse lies limp within the arms of the love-lorn chief.

As he cries out in his woe there are other voices in the cave. First he hears the voice of Ua speaking to him in soothing tones as she stoops to the body of her friend; and then in a little while he hears the voice of his great leader calling to him and bidding him stay his grief. "O King of all the Seas," said Kaaialii, standing up and leaving Kaala to the arms of Ua, "I have lost the flower thou gavest me; it is broken and dead, and I have no more joy in life."

"What!" said Kamehameha, "art thou a chief, and wouldst cast away life for a girl? Here is Ua, who loves thee; she is young and tender like Kaala. Thou shalt have her, and more, if thou dost want. Thou shalt have, besides the land I gave thee in Kohala, all that thou shalt ask of Lanai. Its great valley of Palawai shall be thine; and thou shalt watch my fishing grounds of Kaunolu, and be the Lord of Lanai."

"Hear, O King," said Kaaialii. "I gave to Kaala

more of my life in loving her, and of my strength in seeking for her than ever I gave for thee in battle. I gave to her more of love than I ever gave to my mother, and more of my thought than I ever gave to my own life. She was my very breath, and my life, and how shall I live without her? Her face, since first I saw her, has been ever before me; and her warm breasts were my joy and repose; and now that they are cold to me, I must go where her voice and love have gone. If I shut my eyes now I see her best; therefore let me shut my eyes forevermore." And as he spoke, he stooped to clasp his love, said a tender word of adieu to Ua, and then with a swift, strong blow, crushed in brow and brain with a stone.

The dead chief lay by the side of his love, and Ua wailed over both. Then the King ordered that the two lovers should lie side by side on a ledge of the cave; and that they should be wrapped in tapas which should be brought down through the sea in tight bamboos. Then there was great wailing for the chief and the maid who lay in the cave; and thus wailed Ua:

"Where art thou, O brave chief?
Where art thou, O fond girl?
Will ye sleep by the sound of the sea?
And will ye dream of the gods of the deep?
O sire, where now is thy child?
O mother, where now is thy son?
The lands of Kohala shall mourn,
And valleys of Lanai shall lament.
The spear of the chief shall rot in the cave,
And the tapa of the maid is left undone.
The wreaths for his neck, they shall fade,

They shall fade away on the hills.
O Kaaialii, who shall spear the uku?
O Kaala, who shall gather the na-u?
Have ye gone to the shores of Kahiki,
To the land of our father, Wakea?
Will ye feed on the moss of the cave,
And the limpets of the surf-beaten shore?
O chief, O friend, I would feed ye,
O chief, O friend, I would rest ye.
Ye loved, like the sun and the flower,
Ye lived like the fish and the wave,
And now like the seeds in a shell,
Ye sleep in your cave by the sea.
Alas! O chief, alas! O my friend,
Will ye sleep in the cave evermore?"

And thus Ua wailed, and then was borne away by
her brother to the sorrowful shore of Kaunolu, where
there was loud wailing for the chief and the maid; and
many were the chants of lamentation for the two lovers,
who sleep side by side in the Spouting Cave of Kaala.

XVI

THE TOMB OF PUUPEHE

A LEGEND OF LANAI

FROM "THE HAWAIIAN GAZETTE"

ONE of the interesting localities of tradition, famed in Hawaiian song and story of ancient days, is situate at the southwestern point of the island of Lanai, and known as the *Kupapau o Puupehe*, or Tomb of Puupehe. At the point indicated, on the leeward coast of the island, may be seen a huge block of red lava about eighty feet high and some sixty feet in diameter, standing out in the sea, and detached from the mainland some fifty fathoms, around which centres the following legend.

Observed from the overhanging bluff that overlooks Puupehe, upon the summit of this block or elevated islet, would be noticed a small inclosure formed by a low stone wall. This is said to be the last resting-place of a Hawaiian girl whose body was buried there by her lover Makakehau, a warrior of Lanai.

Puupehe was the daughter of Uaua, a petty chief, one of the dependents of the king of Maui, and she was won by young Makakehau as the joint prize of love and war. These two are described in the *Kani-kau*, or Lamentation, of Puupehe, as mutually captive, the one to the other. The maiden was a sweet flower of Hawaiian beauty. Her glossy brown, spotless body "shone like the clear sun rising out of Haleakala." Her flowing, curly hair, bound by a wreath of lehua blossoms, streamed forth as she ran "like the surf crests scudding before the wind." And the starry eyes of the beautiful daughter of Uaua blinded the young warrior, so that he was called Makakehau, or Misty Eyes.

The Hawaiian brave feared that the comeliness of his dear captive would cause her to be coveted by the chiefs of the land. His soul yearned to keep her all to himself. He said: "Let us go to the clear waters of Kalulu. There we will fish together for the kala and the aku, and there I will spear the turtle. I will hide you, my beloved, forever in the cave of Malauea. Or, we will dwell together in the great ravine of Palawai, where we will eat the young of the uwau bird, and we will bake them in ki leaf with the sweet pala fern root. The ohelo berries of the mountains will refresh my love. We will drink of the cool waters of Maunalei. I will thatch a hut in the thicket of Kaohai for our resting-place, and we shall love on till the stars die."

The meles tell of their love in the Pulou ravine, where they caught the bright iiwi birds, and the scarlet apapani. Ah, what sweet joys in the banana groves of Waiakeakua, where the lovers saw naught so beautiful as themselves! But the "misty eyes" were soon to be made dim by weeping, and dimmer, till the drowning brine should close them forevermore.

Makakehau left his love one day in the cave of Malauea while he went to the mountain spring to fill the water-gourds with sweet water.   This cavern yawns at the base of the overhanging bluff that overtops the rock of Puupehe.   The sea surges far within, but there is an inner space which the expert swimmer can reach, and where Puupehe had often rested and baked the *honu*, or sea turtle, for her absent lover.

This was the season for the *kona*, the terrific storm that comes up from the equator and hurls the ocean in increased volume upon the southern shores of the Hawaiian Islands.   Makakehau beheld from the rock springs of Pulou the vanguard of a great kona,—scuds of rain and thick mist, rushing with a howling wind, across the valley of Palawai.   He knew the storm would fill the cave with the sea and kill his love.   He flung aside his calabashes of water and ran down the steep, then across the great valley and beyond its rim he rushed, through the buffetings of the storm, with an agonized heart, down the hill slope to the shore.

The sea was up indeed.   The yeasty foam of mad surging waves whitened the shore.   The thundering buffet of the charging billows chorused with the howl of the tempest.   Ah! where should Misty Eyes find his love in this blinding storm?   A rushing mountain of sea filled the mouth of Malauea, and the pent-up air hurled back the invading torrent with bubbling roar, blowing forth great streams of spray.   This was a war of matter, a battle of the elements to thrill with pleasure the hearts of strong men.   But with one's

love in the seething gulf of the whirlpool, what would
be to him the sublime cataract?   What, to see amid
the boiling foam the upturned face, and the dear, tender body of one's own and only poor dear love, all
mangled?   *You* might agonize on the brink; but Makakehau sprang into the dreadful pool and snatched his
murdered bride from the jaws of an ocean grave.

The next day, fishermen heard the lamentation of
Makakehau, and the women of the valley came down
and wailed over Puupehe.   They wrapped her in
bright new kapa.   They placed upon her garlands of
the fragrant *na-u* (gardenia).   They prepared her for
burial, and were about to place her in the burial ground
of Manele, but Makakehau prayed that he might be
left alone one night more with his lost love.   And he
was left as he desired.

The next day no corpse nor weeping lover were to be
found, till after some search Makakehau was seen at
work piling up stones on the top of the lone sea tower.
The wondering people of Lanai looked on from the
neighboring bluff, and some sailed around the base of
the columnar rock in their canoes, still wondering,
because they could see no way for him to ascend, for
every face of the rock is perpendicular or overhanging.
The old belief was, that some *akua, kanekoa,* or *keawemauhili* (deities), came at the cry of Makakehau and
helped him with the dead girl to the top.

When Makakehau had finished his labors of placing
his lost love in her grave and placed the last stone
upon it, he stretched out his arms and wailed for
Puupehe, thus:

"Where are you O Puupehe?
  Are you in the cave of Malauea?
  Shall I bring you sweet water,
  The water of the mountain?
  Shall I bring the uwau,
  The pala, and the ohelo?
  Are you baking the honu
  And the red sweet hala?
  Shall I pound the kalo of Maui?
  Shall we dip in the gourd together?
  The bird and the fish are bitter,
  And the mountain water is sour.
  I shall drink it no more;
  I shall drink with Aipuhi,
  The great shark of Manele."

Ceasing his sad wail, Makakehau leaped from the rock into the boiling surge at its base, where his body was crushed in the breakers. The people who beheld the sad scene secured the mangled corpse and buried it with respect in the kupapau of Manele.

XVII

AI KANAKA

A LEGEND OF MOLOKAI

REV. A. O. FORBES

ON the leeward side of the island of Molokai, a little to the east of Kaluaaha lies the beautiful valley of Mapulehu, at the mouth of which is located the *heiau*, or temple, of Iliiliopae, which was erected by direction of Ku-pa, the Moi, to look directly out upon the harbor of Ai-Kanaka, now known as Pukoo. At the time of its construction, centuries ago, Kupa was the *Moi*, or sovereign, of the district embracing the *Ahupuaas*, or land divisions, of Mapulehu and Kaluaaha, and he had his residence in this heiau which was built by him and famed as the largest throughout the whole Hawaiian group.

Kupa had a priest named Kamalo, who resided at Kaluaaha. This priest had two boys, embodiments of mischief, who one day while the King was absent on a fishing expedition, took the opportunity to visit his house at the heiau. Finding there the *pahu kaeke*[1]

---

[1] A species of drum made out of a hollowed section of the trunk of a cocoanut tree and covered over one end with sharkskin. It was generally used in pairs, one larger than the other, somewhat after the idea of the bass and tenor drums of civilized nations. One of these drums was placed on either side of the performer, and the drumming was performed with both hands by tapping with the fingers. By peculiar variations of the

belonging to the temple, they commenced drumming on it.

Some evil-minded persons heard Kamalo's boys drumming on the Kaeke and immediately went and told Kupa that the priest's children were reviling him in the grossest manner on his own drum. This so enraged the King that he ordered his servants to put them to death. Forthwith they were seized and murdered; whereupon Kamalo, their father, set about to secure revenge on the King.

Taking with him a black pig as a present, he started forth to enlist the sympathy and services of the celebrated seer, or wizard, Lanikaula, living some twelve miles distant at the eastern end of Molokai. On the way thither, at the village of Honouli, Kamalo met a man the lower half of whose body had been bitten off by a shark, and who promised to avenge him provided he would slay some man and bring him the lower half of his body to replace his own. But Kamalo, putting no credence in such an offer, pressed on to the sacred grove of Lanikaula. Upon arrival there Lanikaula listened to his grievances but could do nothing for him. He directed him, however, to another prophet, named Kaneakama, at the west end of the island, forty miles distant. Poor Kamalo picked up his pig and travelled back again, past his own home, down the coast to Palaau. Meeting with Kaneakama the prophet directed him to the heiau of Puukahi, at the foot of the *pali*, or precipice, of Kalaupapa, on the

drumming, known only to the initiated, the performer could drum out whatever he wished to express in such a way, it is alleged, as to be intelligible to initiated listeners without uttering a single syllable with the voice.

windward side of the island, where he would find the priest Kahiwakaapuu, who was a *kahu*, or steward, of Kauhuhu, the shark god. Once more the poor man shouldered his pig, wended his way up the long ascent of the hills of Kalae to the pali of Kalaupapa, descending which he presented himself before Kahiwakaapuu, and pleaded his cause. He was again directed to go still farther along the windward side of the island till he should come to the *Ana puhi* (eel's cave), a singular cavern at sea level in the bold cliffs between the valleys of Waikolu and Pelekunu, where Kauhuhu, the shark god, dwelt, and to him he must apply. Upon this away went Kamalo and his pig. Arriving at the cave, he found there Waka and Moo, two kahus of the shark god. "Keep off! Keep off!" they shouted. "This place is kapu. No man can enter here, on penalty of death."

"Death or life," answered he, "it is all the same to me if I can only gain my revenge for my poor boys who have been killed." He then related his story, and his wanderings, adding that he had come to make his appeal to Kauhuhu and cared not for his own life.

"Well," said they to him, "Kauhuhu is away now fishing, but if he finds you here when he returns, our lives as well as yours will pay the forfeit. However, we will see what we can do to help you. We must hide you hereabouts, somewhere, and when he returns trust to circumstances to accomplish your purpose."

But they could find no place to hide him where he would be secure from the search of the god, except the rubbish pile where the offal and scrapings of taro were thrown. They therefore thrust him and his pig into the rubbish heap and covered them over with the taro peelings, enjoining him to keep perfectly still, and watch till he should see eight heavy breakers roll in successively from the sea. He then would know that Kauhuhu was returning from his fishing expedition.

Accordingly, after waiting a while, the eight heavy rollers appeared, breaking successively against the rocks; and sure enough, as the eighth dissolved into foam, the great shark god came ashore. Immediately assuming human form, he began snuffing about the place, and addressing Waka and Moo, his kahus, said to them, "There is a man here." They strenuously denied the charge and protested against the possibility of their allowing such a desecration of the premises. But he was not satisfied. He insisted that there was a man somewhere about, saying, "I smell him, and if I find him you are dead men; if not, you escape." He examined the premises over and over again, never suspecting the rubbish heap, and was about giving up the search when, unfortunately, Kamalo's pig sent forth a squeal which revealed the poor fellow's hiding-place.

Now came the dread moment. The enraged Kauhuhu seized Kamalo with both hands and, lifting him up with the intention of swallowing him, according to his shark instinct, had already inserted the victim's head and shoulders into his mouth before he could speak.

"O Kauhuhu, before you eat me, hear my petition; then do as you like."

"Well for you that you spoke as you did,"

answered Kauhuhu, setting him down again on the ground. "Now, what have you to say? Be quick about it."

Kamalo then rehearsed his grievances and his travels in search for revenge, and presented his pig to the god.

Compassion arose in the breast of Kauhuhu, and he said, "Had you come for any other purpose I would have eaten you, but as your cause is a sacred one I espouse it, and will revenge it on Kupa the King. You must, however, do all that I tell you. Return to the heiau of Puukahi, at the foot of the pali, and take the priest Kahiwakaapuu on your back, and carry him up the pali over to the other side of the island, all the way to your home at Kaluaaha. Erect a sacred fence all around your dwelling-place, and surround it with the sacred flags of white kapa. Collect black hogs by the *lau* (four hundred), red fish by the lau, white fowls by the lau, and bide my coming. Wait and watch till you see a small cloud the size of a man's hand arise, white as snow, over the island of Lanai. That cloud will enlarge as it makes its way across the channel against the wind until it rests on the mountain peaks of Molokai back of Mapulehu Valley. Then a rainbow will span the valley from side to side, whereby you will know that I am there, and that your time of revenge has come. Go now, and remember that you are the only man who ever ventured into the sacred precincts of the great Kauhuhu and returned alive."

Kamalo returned with a joyful heart and performed all that had been commanded him. He built the sacred fence around his dwelling; surrounded the inclosure with sacred flags of white kapa; gathered together black hogs, red fish, and white fowls, each by the lau, as directed, with other articles sacred to the gods, such as cocoanuts and white kapas, and then sat himself down to watch for the promised signs of his revenge. Day after day passed until they multiplied into weeks, and the weeks began to run into months.

Finally, one day, the promised sign appeared. The snow white speck of cloud, no bigger than a man's hand, arose over the mountains of Lanai and made its way across the stormy channel in the face of the opposing gale, increasing as it came, until it settled in a majestic mass on the mountains at the head of Mapulehu Valley. Then appeared a splendid rainbow, proudly over-arching the valley, its ends resting on the high lands on either side. The wind began to blow; the rain began to pour, and shortly a furious storm came down the doomed valley, filling its bed from side to side with a mad rushing torrent, which, sweeping everything before it, spread out upon the belt of lowlands at the mouth of the valley, overwhelming Kupa and all his people in one common ruin, and washing them all into the sea, where they were devoured by the sharks. All were destroyed except Kamalo and his family, who were safe within their sacred inclosure, which the flood dared not touch, though it spread terror and ruin on every side of them. Wherefore the harbor of Pukoo, where this terrible event occurred, was long known as *Ai Kanaka* (man eater), and it has passed into a proverb among the inhabitants of that region that "when the rainbow spans Mapulehu Valley, then look out for the *Waiakoloa*,"—a furious storm of rain and wind which sometimes comes suddenly down that valley.

XVIII

KALIUWAA

SCENE OF THE DEMIGOD KAMAPUAA'S ESCAPE FROM OLOPANA

FROM "THE HAWAIIAN SPECTATOR"

A FEW miles east of Laie, on the windward side of the island of Oahu, are situated the valley and falls of Kaliuwaa, noted as one of the most beautiful and romantic spots of the island, and famed in tradition as possessing more than local interest.

The valley runs back some two miles, terminating abruptly at the foot of the precipitous chain of mountains which runs nearly the whole length of the windward side of Oahu, except for a narrow gorge which affords a channel for a fine brook that descends with considerable regularity to a level with the sea. Leaving his horse at the termination of the valley and entering this narrow pass of not over fifty or sixty feet in width, the traveller winds his way along, crossing and recrossing the stream several times, till he seems to be entering into the very mountain. The walls on each side are of solid rock, from two hundred to three hundred, and in some places four hundred feet high, directly overhead, leaving but a narrow strip of sky visible.

Following up the stream for about a quarter of a

mile, one's attention is directed by the guide to a curiosity called by the natives a *waa* (canoe). Turning to the right, one follows up a dry channel of what once must have been a considerable stream, to the distance of fifty yards from the present stream. Here one is stopped by a wall of solid rock rising perpendicularly before one to the height of some two hundred feet, and down which the whole stream must have descended in a beautiful fall. This perpendicular wall is worn in by the former action of the water in the shape of a gouge, and in the most perfect manner; and as one looks upon it in all its grandeur, but without the presence of the cause by which it was formed, he can scarcely divest his mind of the impression that he is gazing upon some stupendous work of art.

Returning to the present brook, we again pursued our way toward the fall, but had not advanced far before we arrived at another, on the left hand side of the brook, similar in many respects, but much larger and higher than the one above mentioned. The forming agent cannot be mistaken, when a careful survey is made of either of these stupendous perpendicular troughs. The span is considerably wider at the bottom than at the top, this result being produced by the spreading of the sheet of water as it was precipitated from the dizzy height above. The breadth of this one is about twenty feet at the bottom, and its depth about fourteen feet. But its depth and span gradually diminish from the bottom to the top, and the rock is worn as smooth as if chiselled by the hand of an artist. Moss and small plants have sprung out from the little soil that has accumulated in the crevices, but not enough to conceal the rock from observation. It would be an object worth the toil to discover what has turned the stream from its original channel.

Leaving this singular curiosity, we pursued our way a few yards farther, when we arrived at the fall. This is from eighty to one hundred feet high, and the water is compressed into a very narrow space just where it breaks forth from the rock above. It is quite a pretty sheet of water when the stream is high. We learned from the natives that there are two falls above this, both of which are shut out from the view from below, by a sudden turn in the course of the stream. The perpendicular height of each is said to be much greater than of the one we saw. The upper one is visible from the road on the seashore, which is more than two miles distant, and, judging from information obtained, must be between two and three hundred feet high. The impossibility of climbing the perpendicular banks from below deprived us of the pleasure of farther ascending the stream toward its source. This can be done only by commencing at the plain and following up one of the lateral ridges. This would itself be a laborious and fatiguing task, as the way would be obstructed by a thick growth of trees and tangled underbrush.

The path leading to this fall is full of interest to any one who loves to study nature. From where we leave our horses at the head of the valley and commence entering the mountain, every step presents new and peculiar beauties. The most luxuriant verdure clothes the ground, and in some places the beautifully burnished leaves of the ohia, or native apple-tree (*Eugenia malaccensis*), almost exclude the few rays of light that find their way down into this secluded nook. A little farther on, and the graceful bamboo sends up its slender stalk to a great height, mingling its dark, glossy foliage with the silvery leaves of the kukui, or candle-nut (*Aleurites moluccana*); these together form a striking contrast to the black walls which rise in such sullen grandeur on each side.

Nor is the beauty of the spot confined to the luxuriant verdure, or the stupendous walls and beetling crags. The stream itself is beautiful. From the basin at the falls to the lowest point at which we observed it, every succeeding step presents a delightful change. Here, its partially confined waters burst forth with considerable force, and struggle on among the opposing rocks for some distance; there, collected in a little basin, its limpid waves, pure as the drops of dew from the womb of the morning, circle round in ceaseless eddies, until they get within the influence of the downward current, when away they whirl, with a gurgling, happy sound, as if joyous at being released from their temporary confinement. Again, an aged kukui, whose trunk is white with the moss of accumulated years, throws his broad boughs far over the stream that nourishes his vigorous roots, casting a meridian shadow upon the surface of the water, which is reflected back with singular distinctness from its mirrored bosom.

To every other gratification must be added the incomparable fragrance of the fresh wood, in perpetual life and vigor, which presents a freshness truly grateful to the senses. But it is in vain to think of conveying an adequate idea of a scene where the sublime is mingled with the beautiful, and the bold and striking with the delicate and sensitive; where every sense is gratified, the mind calmed, and the whole soul delighted.

Famed as this spot is for its natural scenic attractions, intimated in the foregoing description, its claim of distinction with Hawaiians is indelibly fixed by the traditions of ancient times, the narration of which, at this point, will assist the reader to understand the character of the native mind and throw some light also on the history of the Hawaiians.

Tradition in this locality deals largely with Kamapuaa, the famous demigod whose exploits figure prominently in the legends of the entire group. Summarized, the story is about as follows:

Kamapuaa, the fabulous being referred to, seems, according to the tradition, to have possessed the power of transforming himself into a hog, in which capacity he committed all manner of depredations upon the possessions of his neighbors. He having stolen some fowls belonging to Olopana, who was the King of Oahu, the latter, who was then living at Kaneohe, sent some of his men to secure the thief. They succeeded in capturing him, and having tied him fast with cords, were bearing him in triumph to the King, when, thinking they had carried the joke far enough, he burst the bands with which he was bound, and killed all the men except one, whom he permitted to

convey the tidings to the King. This defeat so
enraged the monarch that he determined to go in person with all his force, and either destroy his enemy, or
drive him from his dominions. He accordingly, des-
pising ease inglorious,

> Waked up, with sound of conch and trumpet shell,
> The well-tried warriors of his native dell,

at whose head he sought his waiting enemy. Success
attending the King's attack, his foe was driven from
the field with great loss, and betook himself to the
gorge of Kaliuwaa, which leads to the falls. Here the
King thought he had him safe; and one would think
so too, to look at the immense precipices that rise on
each side, and the falls in front. But the sequel will
show that he had a slippery fellow to deal with, at
least when he chose to assume the character of a swine;
for, being pushed to the upper end of the gorge near
the falls, and seeing no other way of escape, he suddenly transformed himself into a hog, and, rearing
upon his hind legs and leaning his back against the
perpendicular precipice, thus afforded a very comfort-
able ladder upon which the remnant of his army
ascended and made their escape from the vengeance
of the King. Possessing such powers, it is easy to see
how he could follow the example of his soldiers and
make his own escape. The smooth channels before
described are said to have been made by him on these
occasions; for he was more than once caught in the
same predicament. Old natives still believe that they
are the prints of his back; and they account for a very

natural phenomenon, by bringing to their aid this most natural and foolish superstition.

Many objects in the neighborhood are identified with this remarkable personage, such as a large rock to which he was tied, a wide place in the brook where he used to drink, and a number of trees he is said to have planted. Many other things respecting him are current, but as they do not relate to the matter in hand, it will perhaps suffice to say, in conclusion, that tradition further asserts that Kamapuaa conquered the volcano, when Pele its goddess became his wife, and that they afterward lived together in harmony. That is the reason why there are no more islands formed, or very extensive eruptions in these later days, as boiling lava was the most potent weapon she used in fighting her enemies, throwing out such quantities as greatly to increase the size of the islands, and even to form new ones.

Visitors to the falls, even to this day, meet with evidences of the superstitious awe in which the locality is held by the natives. A party who recently visited the spot states that when they reached the falls they were instructed to make an offering to the presiding goddess. This was done in true Hawaiian style; they built a tiny pile of stones on one or two large leaves, and so made themselves safe from falling stones, which otherwise would assuredly have struck them.

XIX

BATTLE OF THE OWLS

JOS. M. POEPOE

THE following is a fair specimen of the animal myths current in ancient Hawaii, and illustrates the place held by the owl in Hawaiian mythology.

There lived a man named Kapoi, at Kahehuna, in Honolulu, who went one day to Kewalo to get some thatching for his house. On his way back he found some owl's eggs, which he gathered together and brought home with him. In the evening he wrapped them in ti leaves and was about to roast them in hot ashes, when an owl perched on the fence which surrounded his house and called out to him, "O Kapoi, give me my eggs!"

Kapoi asked the owl, "How many eggs had you?"

"Seven eggs," replied the owl.

Kapoi then said, "Well, I wish to roast these eggs for my supper."

The owl asked the second time for its eggs, and was answered by Kapoi in the same manner. Then said the owl, "O heartless Kapoi! why don't you take pity on me? Give me my eggs."

Kapoi then told the owl to come and take them.

The owl, having got the eggs, told Kapoi to build up a *heiau*, or temple, and instructed him to make an altar and call the temple by the name of Manua. Kapoi built the temple as directed; set kapu days for its dedication, and placed the customary sacrifice on the altar.

News spread to the hearing of Kakuihewa, who was then King of Oahu, living at the time at Waikiki, that a certain man had kapued certain days for his heiau, and had already dedicated it. This King had made a law that whoever among his people should erect a heiau and kapu the same before the King had his temple kapued, that man should pay the penalty of death. Kapoi was thereupon seized, by the King's orders, and led to the heiau of Kupalaha, at Waikiki.

That same day, the owl that had told Kapoi to erect a temple gathered all the owls from Lanai, Maui, Molokai, and Hawaii to one place at Kalapueo.[1] All those from the Koolau districts were assembled at Kanoniakapueo,[2] and those from Kauai and Niihau at Pueohulunui, near Moanalua.

It was decided by the King that Kapoi should be put to death on the day of Kane.[3] When that day came, at daybreak the owls left their places of rendezvous and covered the whole sky over Honolulu; and as the King's servants seized Kapoi to put him to death, the owls flew at them, pecking them with their beaks and scratching them with their claws. Then and there was fought the battle between Kakuihewa's people and the owls. At last the owls conquered, and

---

[1] Situate beyond Diamond Head.

[2] In Nuuanu Valley.

[3] When the moon is twenty-seven days old.

Kapoi was released, the King acknowledging that his *Akua* (god) was a powerful one.   From that time the owl has been recognized as one of the many deities venerated by the Hawaiian people.

XX

THIS LAND IS THE SEA'S

TRADITIONAL ACCOUNT OF AN ANCIENT HAWAIIAN PROPHECY

TRANSLATED FROM MOKE MANU BY THOS. G. THRUM

IT is stated in the history of Kaopulupulu that he was famed among the kahunas of the island of Oahu for his power and wisdom in the exercise of his profession, and was known throughout the land as a leader among the priests. His place of residence was at Waimea, between Koolauloa and Waialua, Oahu. There he married, and there was born to him a son whom he named Kahulupue, and whom he instructed during his youth in all priestly vocations.

In after years when Kumahana, brother of Kahahana of Maui, became the governing chief (*alii aimoku*) of Oahu, Kahulupue was chosen by him as his priest. This chief did evil unto his subjects, seizing their property and beheading and maiming many with the *leiomano* (shark's tooth weapon) and *pahoa* (dagger), without provocation, so that he became a reproach to his people. From such treatment Kahulupue endeavored to dissuade him, assuring him that such a course would fail to win their support and obedience, whereas the supplying of food and fish, with covering

for the body, and malos, would insure their affection-
ate regard. The day of the people was near, for the
time of conflict was approaching when he would meet
the enemy. But these counsels of Kahulupue were
disregarded, so he returned to his father at Waimea.

Not long thereafter this chief Kumahana was cast
out and rejected by the lesser chiefs and people, and
under cover of night he escaped by canoe to Molokai,
where he was ignored and became lost to further history
in consequence of his wrong-doings.

When Kahekili, King of Maui, heard of the stealthy
flight of the governing chief of Oahu, he placed the
young prince Kahahana, his foster-son, as ruler over
Oahu in the place of his deposed relative, Kumahana.
This occurred about the year 1773, and Kahahana
took with him as his intimate friend and companion
one Alapai. Kahahana chose as his place of residence
the shade of the kou and cocoanut trees of Ulukou,
Waikiki, where also gathered together the chiefs of the
island to discuss and consider questions of state.

The new ruler being of fine and stalwart form and
handsome appearance, the chiefs and common people
maintained that his fame in this respect induced a celebrated chieftainess of Kauai, named Kekuapoi, to voyage hither. Her history, it is said, showed that she
alone excelled in maiden charm and beauty; she was
handsome beyond all other chiefesses from Hawaii
to Kauai, as "the third brightness of the sun" (*he ekolu
ula o ka la*). In consequence, Kahahana took her as
his wife, she being own sister to Kekuamanoha.

At this time the thought occurred to the King to

inquire through the chiefs of Oahu of the whereabouts of Kaopulupulu, the celebrated priest, of whom he had heard through Kahekili, King of Maui.   In reply to this inquiry of Kahahana, the chiefs told him that his place of residence was at Waimea, whereupon a messenger was sent to bid him come up by order of the King.   When the messenger reached Kaopulupulu he delivered the royal order.   Upon the priest hearing this word of the King he assented thereto, with this reply to the messenger: "You return first and tell him that on the morning after the fourteenth night of the moon (*po o akua*), I will reach the place of the King."

At the end of the conference the messenger returned and stood before Kahahana and revealed the words of Kaopulupulu; and the King waited for the time of his arrival.

It is true, Kaopulupulu made careful preparation for his future.   Toward the time of his departure he was engaged in considering the good or evil of his approaching journey by the casting of lots, according to the rites of his profession.   He foresaw thereby the purpose of the King in summoning him to dwell at court.   He therefore admonished his son to attend to all the rites and duties of the priesthood as he had been taught, and to care for his mother and relatives.

At early dawn Kaopulupulu arose and partook of food till satisfied, after which he prepared himself for the journey before him.   After he had given his farewell greetings to his household he seized his bundle and, taking a cocoanut fan in his hand, set out toward Punanue, where was a temple (*heiau*) for priests only,

called Kahokuwelowelo. This was crown land at Waialua in ancient times. Entering the temple he prayed
for success in his journey, after which he proceeded
along the plains of Lauhulu till reaching the Anahulu
stream, thence by Kemoo to Kukaniloko, the shelter
of whose prominent rock the chiefesses of Oahu were
wont to choose for their place of confinement.

Leaving this place he came to Kalakoa, where
Kekiopilo the prophet priest lived and died, and the
scene of his vision at high noon when he prophesied
of the coming of foreigners with a strange language.
Here he stopped and rested with some of the people,
and ate food with them, after which he journeyed on
by way of Waipio by the ancient path of that time till
he passed Ewa and reached Kapukaki.

The sun was well up when he reached the water of
Lapakea, so he hastened his steps in ascending Kau-
walua, at Moanalua, and paused not till he came to
the mouth of the Apuakehau stream at Waikiki.
Proceeding along the sand at this place he was dis-
cerned by the retainers of the King and greeted with
the shout, "Here comes the priest Kaopulupulu."

When the King heard this he was exceedingly
pleased (*pihoihoi loa*) at the time, and on the priest's
meeting with King Kahahana he welcomed Kaopulupulu with loud rejoicing.

Without delay the King set apart a house wherein
to meet and discuss with the priest those things he
had in mind, and in the consideration of questions
from first to last, Kaopulupulu replied with great
wisdom in accordance with his knowledge of his pro-

fession.   At this time of their conference he sat within the doorway of the house, and the sun was near its setting.   As he turned to observe this he gazed out into the sky and noticing the gathering short clouds (*ao poko*) in the heavens, he exclaimed:

"O heaven, the road is broad for the King, it is full of chiefs and people; narrow is my path, that of the kahuna; you will not be able to find it, O King. Even now the short clouds reveal to me the manner of your reign; it will not be many days.   Should you heed my words, O King, you will live to gray hair. But you will be the king to slay me and my child."

At these words of the priest the King meditated seriously for some time, then spoke as follows: "Why should my days be short, and why should your death be by me, the King?"

Kaopulupulu replied: "O King, let us look into the future.   Should you die, O King, the lands will be desolate; but for me, the kahuna, the name will live on from one generation to another; but my death will be before thine, and when I am up on the heaven-feared altar then my words will gnaw thee, O King, and the rains and the sun will bear witness."

These courageous words of Kaopulupulu, spoken in the presence of Kahahana without fear, and regardless of the dignity and majesty of the King, were uttered because of the certainty that the time would come when his words would be carried into effect. The King remained quiet without saying a word, keeping his thoughts to himself.

After this conference the King took Kaopulupulu

to be his priest, and in course of time he became also an intimate companion, in constant attendance upon the King, and counselled him in the care of his subjects, old and young, in all that pertained to their welfare. The King regarded his words, and in their circuit of the island together they found the people contented and holding their ruler in high esteem. But at the end of three years the King attempted some wrong to certain of his subjects like unto that of his deposed predecessor. The priest remonstrated with him continually, but he would not regard his counsel; therefore, Kaopulupulu left King Kahahana and returned to his land at Waimea and at once tattooed his knees. This was done as a sign that the King had turned a deaf ear to his admonitions.

When several days had passed, rumors among certain people of Waialua reached the priest that he was to be summoned to appear before the King in consequence of this act, which had greatly angered his august lord. Kahahana had gone to reside at Waianae, and from there shortly afterward he sent messengers to fetch Kaopulupulu and his son Kahulupue from Waimea.

In the early morning of the day of the messenger's arrival, a rainbow stood directly in the doorway of Kaopulupulu's house, and he asked of his god its meaning; but his prayer was broken (*ua haki ka pule*). This boded him ill; therefore he called to his son to stand in prayer; but the result was the same. Then he said, "This augurs of the day of death; see! the rising up of a man in the pass of Hapuu, putting on his kapa with its knot fastening on the left side of the neck, which means that he is bringing a death message."

Shortly after the priest had ended these words a man was indeed seen approaching along the mountain pass, with his kapa as indicated; and he came and stood before the door of their house and delivered the order of the King for them to go to Waianae, both him and his son.

The priest replied: "Return you first; we will follow later," and the messenger obeyed. When he had departed Kaopulupulu recalled to his son the words he had spoken before the advent of the messenger, and said: "Oh, where are you, my child? Go clothe the body; put on the malo; eat of the food till satisfied, and we will go as commanded by the King; but this journey will result in placing us on the altar (*kau i ka lele*). Fear not death. The name of an idler, if he be beaten to death, is not passed on to distinction."

At the end of these words of his father, Kahulupue wept for love of his relatives, though his father bid him to weep not for his family, because he, Kaopulupulu, saw the end that would befall the King, Kahahana, and his court of chiefs and retainers. Even at this time the voices of distress were heard among his family and their tears flowed, but Kaopulupulu looked on unmoved by their cries.

He then arose and, with his son, gave farewell greetings to their household, and set forth. In journeying they passed through Waialua, resting in the house of a kamaaina at Kawaihapai. In passing the night at this place Kahulupue slept not, but went out to examine the fishing canoes of that neighborhood. Finding a large one suitable for a voyage, he returned and awoke his father, that they might flee together that night to Kauai and dwell on the knoll of Kalalea. But Kaopulupulu declined the idea of flight. In the morning, ascending a hill, they turned and looked back over the sea-spray of Waialua to the swimming halas of Kahuku beyond. Love for the place of his birth so overcame Kaopulupulu for a time that his tears flowed for that he should see it no more.

Then they proceeded on their way till, passing Kaena Point, they reached the temple of Puaakanoe. At this sacred boundary Kaopulupulu said to his son, "Let us swim in the sea and touch along the coast of Makua." At one of their resting-places, journeying thus, he said, with direct truthfulness, as his words proved: "Where are you, my son? For this drenching of the high priests by the sea, seized will be the sacred lands (*moo-kapu*) from Waianae to Kualoa by the chief from the east."

As they were talking they beheld the King's men approaching along the sand of Makua, and shortly afterward these men came before them and seized them and tied their hands behind their backs and took them to the place of King Kahahana at Puukea, Waianae, and put them, father and son, in a new grass hut unfinished of its ridge thatch, and tied them, the one to the end post (*pouhana*) and the other to the corner post (*poumanu*) of the house.

At the time of the imprisonment of the priest and his son in this new house Kaopulupulu spake aloud, without fear of dire consequences, so that the King and all his men heard him, as follows: "Here I am with my son in this new unfinished house; so will be unfinished the reign of the King that slays us." At this saying Kahahana, the King, was very angry.

Throughout that day and the night following, till the sun was high with warmth, the King was directing his soldiers to seize Kahulupue first and put him to death. Obeying the orders of the King, they took Kahulupue just outside of the house and stabbed at his eyes with laumake spears and stoned him with stones before the eyes of his father, with merciless cruelty. These things, though done by the soldiers, were dodged by Kahulupue, and the priest, seeing the King had no thought of regard for his child, spoke up with priestly authority, as follows: "Be strong of breath, my son, till the body touch the water, for the land indeed is the sea's."

When Kahulupue heard the voice of his father telling him to flee to the sea, he turned toward the shore in obedience to these last words to him, because of the attack by the soldiers of the King. As he ran, he was struck in the back by a spear, but he persevered and leaped into the sea at Malae and was drowned, his blood discoloring the water. His dead body was taken and placed up in the temple at Puehuehu. After the kapu days therefore the King, with his chiefs and soldiers, moved to Puuloa, Ewa, bringing with them the priest Kaopulupulu, and after some days

he was brought before the King by the soldiers, and
without groans for his injuries was slain in the King's
presence.   But he spoke fearlessly of the vengeance
that would fall upon the King in consequence of his
death, and during their murderous attack upon him
proclaimed with his dying breath: "You, O King,
that kill me here at Puuloa, the time is near when a
direct death will be yours.   Above here in this land,
and the spot where my lifeless body will be borne and
placed high on the altar for my flesh to decay and slip
to the earth, shall be the burial place of chiefs and
people hereafter, and it shall be called 'the royal sand
of the mistaken'; there will you be placed in the
temple."   At the end of these words of Kaopulupulu
his spirit took flight, and his body was left for mockery
and abuse, as had been that of his son in the sea of
Malae, at Waianae.

After a while the body of the priest was placed on
a double canoe and brought to Waikiki and placed high
in the cocoanut trees at Kukaeunahi, the place of the
temple, for several ten-day periods (*he mau anahulu*)
without decomposition and falling off of the flesh to
the sands of Waikiki.

When King Kahekili of Maui heard of the death
of the priest Kaopulupulu by Kahahana, he sent some
of his men thither by canoe, who landed at Waiman-
alo, Koolau, where, as spies, they learned from the
people respecting Kaopulupulu and his death, with
that of his son; therefore they returned and told the
King the truth of these reports, at which the affection
of Kahekili welled up for the dead priest, and he con-

demned the King he had established. Coming with an army from Maui, he landed at Waikiki without meeting Kahahana, and took back the government of Oahu under his own kingship. The chiefs and people of Oahu all joined under Kahekili, for Kahahana had been a chief of wrong-doing. This was the first sea of Kaopulupulu in accordance with his prophetic utterance to his son, "This land is the sea's."

Upon the arrival here at Oahu of Kahekili, Kahahana fled, with his wife Kekuapoi, and friend Alapai, and hid in the shrubbery of the hills. They went to Aliomanu, Moanalua, to a place called Kinimakalehua; then moved along to Keanapuaa and Kepookala, at the lochs of Puuloa, and from there to upper Waipio; thence to Wahiawa, Helemano, and on to Lihue; thence they came to Poohilo, at Honouliuli, where they first showed themselves to the people and submitted themselves to their care.

While they were living there, report thereof was made to Kahekili, the King, who thereupon sent Kekuamanoha, elder brother of Kekuapoi, the wife of Kahahana, with men in double canoes from Waikiki, landing first at Kupahu, Hanapouli, Waipio, with instructions to capture and put to death Kahahana, as also his friend Alapai, but to save alive Kekuapoi. When the canoes touched at Hanapouli, they proceeded thence to Waikele and Hoaeae, and from there to Poohilo, Honouliuli, where they met in conference with Kahahana and his party. At the close of the day Kekuamanoha sought by enticing words to induce his brother-in-law to go up with him and see the father

King and be assured of no death condemnation, and by skilled flattery he induced Kahahana to consent to his proposition; whereupon preparation was made for the return. On the following morning, coming along and reaching the plains of Hoaeae, they fell upon and slew Kahahana and Alapai there, and bore their lifeless bodies to Halaulani, Waipio, where they were placed in the canoes and brought up to Waikiki and placed up in the cocoanut trees by King Kahekili and his priests from Maui, as Kaopulupulu had been. Thus was fulfilled the famous saying of the Oahu priest in all its truthfulness.

According to the writings of S. M. Kamakau and David Malo, recognized authorities, the thought of Kaopulupulu as expressed to his son Kahulupue, "This land is the sea's," was in keeping with the famous prophetic vision of Kekiopilo that "the foreigners possess the land," as the people of Hawaii now realize. The weighty thought of this narration and the application of the saying of Kaopulupulu to this time of enlightenment are frequent with certain leaders of thought among the people, as shown in their papers.

XXI

KU-ULA, THE FISH GOD OF HAWAII

TRANSLATED FROM MOKE MANU BY M. K. NAKUINA

THE story of Ku-ula, considered by ancient Hawaiians as the deity presiding over and controlling the fish of the sea,—a story still believed by many of them to-day,—is translated and somewhat condensed from an account prepared by a recognized legendary bard of these islands. The name of Ku-ula is known from the ancient times on each of the islands of the Hawaiian group, and the writer gives the Maui version as transmitted through the old people of that island.

Ku-ula had a human body, and was possessed with wonderful or miraculous power (*mana kupua*) in directing, controlling, and influencing all fish of the sea, at will.

Leho-ula, in the land of Aleamai, Hana, Maui, is where Ku-ula and Hina-pu-ku-ia lived. Nothing is known of their parents, but tradition deals with Ku-ula, his wife, their son Ai-ai, and Ku-ula-uka, a younger brother of Ku-ula. These lived together for a time at Leho-ula, and then the brothers divided their work between them, Ku-ula-uka choosing farm work, or work pertaining to the land, from the sea-shore to the mountain-top, while Ku-ula—known also

as Ku-ula-kai—chose to be a fisherman, with such other
work as pertained to the sea, from the pebbly shore to
ocean depths. After this division Ku-ula-uka went
up in the mountains to live, and met a woman known
as La-ea—called also Hina-ulu-ohia—a sister of Hina-
pu-ku-ia, Ku-ula's wife. These sisters had three
brothers, named Moku-ha-lii, Kupa-ai-kee, and
Ku-pulu-pulu-i-ka-na-hele. This trio were called by
the old people the gods of the canoe-making priests
—"*Na akua aumakua o ka poe kahuna kalai waa.*"

While Ku-ula and his wife were living at Leho-ula
he devoted all his time to his chosen vocation, fishing.
His first work was to construct a fish-pond handy to
his house but near to the shore where the surf breaks,
and this pond he stocked with all kinds of fish. Upon
a rocky platform he also built a house to be sacred for
the fishing kapu which he called by his own name,
Ku-ula.

It is asserted that when Ku-ula made all these preparations he believed in the existence of a God who had
supreme power over all things. That is why he prepared this place wherein to make his offerings of the
first fish caught by him to the fish god. From this
observance of Ku-ula all the fish were tractable (*laka
loa*) unto him; all he had to do was to say the word,
and the fish would appear. This was reported all
over Hana and when Kamohoalii the King (who
was then living at Wananalua, the land on which
Kauiki Hill stands) heard of it, he appointed Ku-ula
to be his head fisherman. Through this pond, which
was well stocked with all kinds of fish, the King's

table was regularly supplied with all rare varieties, whether in or out of season. Ku-ula was his main-stay for fish-food and was consequently held in high esteem by Kamohoalii, and they lived without dis-agreement of any kind between them for many years.

During this period the wife of Ku-ula gave birth to a son, whom they called Aiai-a-Ku-ula (Aiai of Ku-ula). The child was properly brought up accord-ing to the usage of those days, and when he was old enough to care for himself an unusual event occurred.

A large *puhi* (eel), called Koona, lived at Wailau, on the windward side of the island of Molokai. This eel was deified and prayed to by the people of that place, and they never tired telling of the mighty things their god did, one of which was that a big shark came to Wailau and gave it battle, and during the fight the puhi caused a part of the rocky cliff to fall upon the shark, which killed it. A cave was thus formed, with a depth of about five fathoms; and that large opening is there to this day, situate a little above the sea and close to the rocky fort where lived the well known Kapepeekauila. This puhi then left its own place and came and lived in a cave in the sea near Aleamai, called Kapukaulua, some distance out from the Alau rocks. It came to break and rob the pond that Ku-ula had built and stocked with fish of various kinds and colors, as known to-day.

Ku-ula was much surprised on discovering his pond stock disappearing, so he watched day and night, and at last, about daybreak, he saw a large eel come in through the *makai* (seaward) wall of the pond. When he saw this he knew that it was the cause of the loss of his fish, and was devising a way to catch and kill it; but on consulting with his wife they decided to leave the matter to their son Aiai, for him to use his own judgment as to the means by which the thief might be captured and killed. When Aiai was told of it he sent word to all the people of Aleamai and Haneoo to make ili hau ropes several lau fathoms in length; and when all was ready a number of the people went out with it in two canoes, one each from the two places, with Aiai-a-Ku-ula in one of them. He put two large stones in his canoe and held in his hands a fisherman's gourd (*hokeo*), in which was a large fish-hook called manaiaakalani.

When the canoes had proceeded far out he located his position by landmarks; and looking down into the sea, and finding the right place, he told the paddlers to cease paddling. Standing up in the canoe and taking one of the stones in his hands he dived into the sea. Its weight took him down rapidly to the bottom, where he saw a big cave opening right before him, with a number of fishes scurrying about the entrance, such as uluas and other deep sea varieties. Feeling assured thereby that the puhi was within, he arose to the surface and got into his canoe. Resting for a moment, he then opened the gourd and took out the hook manaiaakalani and tied the hau rope to it. He also picked up a long stick and placed at the end of it the hook, baited with a preparation of cocoanut and other substances attractive to fishes. Before taking his second dive he arranged with those on the canoe as to the signs to them of his

success.   Saying this, he picked up the other stone and
dived down again into the sea; then, proceeding to the
cave, he placed the hook in it, at the same time mur-
muring a few incantations in the name of his parents.
When he knew that the puhi was hooked he signalled,
as planned, to tell those on the canoe of his success.
In a short while he came to the surface, and entering
the canoe they all returned to shore, trailing the rope
behind.   He told those in the canoe from Haneoo to
paddle thither and to Hamoa, and to tell all the people
to pull the puhi; like instructions were given those on
the Aleamai canoe for their people.   The two canoes
set forth on their courses to the landings, keeping in
mind Aiai's instructions, which were duly carried out
by the people of the two places; and there were many
for the work.

Then Aiai ascended Kaiwiopele Hill and motioned
to the people of both places to pull the ropes attached
to the hook on the mouth of the puhi.   It was said
that the Aleamai people won the victory over the much
greater number from the other places, by landing the
puhi on the pahoehoe stones at Lehoula.   The people
endeavored to kill the prize, but without success till
Aiai came and threw three ala stones at it and killed
it.   The head was cut off and cooked in the *imu* (oven).
The bones of its jaw, with the mouth wide open, are
seen to this day at a place near the shore, washed by
the waves,—the rock formation at a short distance
having such a resemblance.

Residents of the place state that all ala stones near
where the imu was made in which the puhi was baked

do not crack when heated, as they do elsewhere, because of the imu heating of that time. It is so even to this day. The backbone (*iwi kuamoo*) of this puhi is still lying on the pahoehoe where Aiai killed it with the three ala stones,—the rocky formation, about thirty feet in length, exactly resembling the backbone of an eel. The killing of this puhi by Aiai gave him fame among the people of Hana. Its capture was the young lad's first attempt to follow his father's vocation, and his knowledge was a surprise to the people.

After this event a man came over from Wailau, Molokai, who was a *kahu* (keeper) of the puhi. He dreamed one night that he saw its spirit, which told him that his *aumakua* (god) had been killed at Hana, so he came to see with his own eyes where this had occurred. Arriving at Wananalua he was befriended by one of the retainers of Kamohoalii, the King of Hana, and lived there a long time serving under him, during which time he learned the story of how the puhi had been caught and killed by Aiai, the son of Ku-ula and Hinapukuia, whereupon he sought to accomplish their death.

Considering a plan of action, he went one day to Ku-ula, without orders, and told him that the King had sent him for fish for the King. Ku-ula gave him but one fish, an ulua, with a warning direction, saying, "Go back to the King and tell him to cut off the head of the fish and cook it in the imu, and the flesh of its body cut up and salt and dry in the sun, for 'this is Hana the *aupehu* land; Hana of the scarce fish; the fish Kama; the fish of Lanakila.' (*Eia o Hana la he aina aupehu; o Hana keia i ka ia iki; ka ia o Kama; ka ia o Lanakila*)."

When the man returned to the King and gave him the fish, the King asked: "Who gave it to you?" and the man answered:

"Ku-ula."

Then it came into his head that this was his chance for revenge, so he told the King what Ku-ula had said but not in the same way, saying: "Your head fisherman told me to come back and tell you that your head should be cut from your body and cooked in the imu, and the flesh of your body should be cut up and salted and dried in the sun."

The King on hearing this message was so angered with Ku-ula, his head fisherman, that he told the man to go and tell all his *konohikis* (head men of lands with others under them) and people, to go up in the mountains and gather immediately plenty of firewood and place it around Ku-ula's house, for he and his wife and child should be burned up.

This order of the King was carried out by the konohikis and people of all his lands except those of Aleamai. These latter did not obey this order of the King, for Ku-ula had always lived peaceably among them. There were days when they had no fish, and he had supplied them freely.

When Ku-ula and his wife saw the people of Hana bringing firewood and placing it around the house they knew it foreboded trouble; so Ku-ula went to a place where taro, potatoes, bananas, cane, and some gourds were growing. Seeing three dry gourds on the vine, he asked the owner for them and was told to take them. These he took to his house and discussed with his wife the evil day to come, and told Aiai that their house would be burned and their bodies too, but not to fear death nor trouble himself about it when the people came to shut them in.

After some thinking Ku-ula remembered his giving the ulua to the King's retainer and felt that he was the party to blame for this action of the King's people. He had suspected it before, but now felt sure; therefore he turned to his son and said: "Our child, Aiai-a-Ku-ula, if our house is burned, and our bodies too, you must look sharp for the smoke when it goes straight up to the hill of Kaiwiopele. That will be your way out of this trouble, and you must follow it till you find a cave where you will live. You must take this hook called manaiaakalani with you; also this fish-pearl (*pa hi aku*), called *Kahuoi;* this shell called *lehoula*, and this small sandstone from which I got the name they call me, *Ku-ula-au-a-Ku-ulakai*. It is the progenitor of all the fish in the sea. You will be the one to make all the ku-ulas from this time forth, and have charge also of making all the fishing stations (*ko'a lawaia*) in the sea throughout the islands. Your name shall be perpetuated and those of your parents also, through all generations to come, and I hereby confer upon you all my power and knowledge. Whenever you desire anything call, or ask, in our names, and we will grant it. We will stand up and go forth from here into the sea and abide there forever; and you, our child, shall live on the land here without worrying about anything that may happen to you. You will have power to punish with death all those who have helped to burn us and our house. Whether it be king or people, they must die; therefore let us calmly await the calamity that is to befall us."

All these instructions Aiai consented to carry out from first to last, as a dutiful son.

After Ku-ula's instructions to his son, consequent upon the manifestations of coming trouble, the King's people came one day and caught them and tied their hands behind their backs, the evil-doer from Molokai being there to aid in executing the cruel orders of Kamohoalii resulting from his deceitful story. Upon being taken into their house Ku-ula was tied to the end post of the ridge pole (*pouhana*), the wife was tied to the middle post (*kai waena*) of the house, and the boy, Aiai, was tied to one of the corner posts (*pou o manu*). Upon fastening them in this manner the people went out of the house and barricaded the doorway with wood, which they then set on fire. Before the fire was lit, the ropes with which the victims were tied dropped off from their hands. Men, women, and children looked on at the burning house with deep pity for those within, and tears were streaming down their cheeks as they remembered the kindness of Ku-ula during all the time they had lived together. They knew not why this family and their house should be burned in this manner.

When the fire was raging all about the house and the flames were consuming everything, Ku-ula and his wife gave their last message to their son and left him.

They went right out of the house as quietly as the last
breath leaves the body, and none of the people standing there gazing saw where, or how, Ku-ula and his
wife came forth out of the house.   Aiai was the only
one that retained material form.   Their bodies were
changed by some miraculous power and entered the sea,
taking with them all the fish swimming in and around
Hana.   They also took all sea-mosses, crabs, crawfish,
and the various kinds of shellfish along the seashore,
even to the opihi-koele at the rocky beach; every edible thing in the sea was taken away.   This was the first
stroke of Ku-ula's revenge on the King and the people
of Hana who obeyed his mandate; they suffered greatly
from the scarcity of fish.

When Ku-ula and his wife were out of the house the
three gourds exploded from the heat, one by one, and
all those who were gazing at the burning house believed
the detonations indicated the bursting of the bodies of
Ku-ula, his wife, and child.   The flames shot up
through the top of the house, and the black smoke hov-
ered above it, then turned toward the front of Kaiwiopele Hill.   The people saw Aiai ascend through the
flames and walk upon the smoke toward the hill till
he came to a small cave that opened to receive and
rescue him.

As Aiai left the house it burned fiercely, and, carrying out the instructions of his father he called upon
him to destroy by fire all those who had caught and
tied them in their burning house.   As he finished
his appeal he saw the rippling of the wind on the sea
and a misty rain coming with it, increasing as it came

till it reached Lehoula, which so increased the blazing of the fire that the flames reached out into the crowd of people for those who had obeyed the King. The man from Molokai, who was the cause of the trouble, was reached also and consumed by the fire, and the charred bodies were left to show to the people the second stroke of Ku-ula's vengeance. Strange to say, all those who had nothing to do with this cruel act, though closer to the burning house, were uninjured; the tongues of fire reached out only for the guilty ones. In a little while but a few smouldering logs and ashes were all that remained of the house of Ku-ula. Owing to this strange action of the fire some of the people doubted the death of Ku-ula and his wife, and much disputation arose among them on the subject.

When Aiai walked out through the flames and smoke and reached the cave, he stayed there through that night till the next morning, then, leaving his hook, pearl shell, and stone there, he went forth till he came to the road at Puilio, where he met several children amusing themselves by shooting arrows, one of whom made friends with him and asked him to his house. Aiai accepted the invitation, and the boy and his parents treating him well, he remained with them for some days.

While Aiai was living in their house the parents of the boy heard of the King's order for all the people of Hana to go fishing for hinalea. The people obeyed the royal order, but when they went down to the shore with their fishing baskets they looked around for the usual bait (*ueue*), which was to be pounded up and put into the baskets, but they could not find any, nor any other material to be so used, neither could they see any fish swimming around in the sea. "Why?" was the question. Because Ku-ula and his wife had taken with them all the fish and everything pertaining to fishing. Finding no bait they pounded up limestone and placed it in the baskets and swam out and set them in the sea. They watched and waited all day, but in vain, for not a single hinalea was seen, nor did any enter the baskets. When night came they went back empty-handed and came down again the next day only to meet the same luck. The parents of the boy who had befriended Aiai were in this fishing party, in obedience to the King's orders, but they got nothing for their trouble. Aiai, seeing them go down daily to Haneoo, asked concerning it, and was told everything; so he bade his friend come with him to the cave where he had stayed after his father's house was burned. Arriving there he showed the stone fish god, Pohaku-muone, and said: "We can get fish up here from this stone without much work or trouble."

Then Aiai picked up the stone and they went down to Lehoula, and setting it down at a point facing the pond which his father had made he repeated these words: "O Ku-ula, my father; O Hina, my mother, I place this stone here in your name, Ku-ula, which action will make your name famous and mine too, your son; the keeping of this ku-ula stone I give to my friend, and he and his offspring hereafter will do and act in all things pertaining to it in our names."

After saying these words he told his friend his duties

and all things to be observed relative to the stone and
the benefits to be derived therefrom as an influencing
power over such variety of fish as he desired.   This
was the first establishment of the *ko'a ku-ula* on land,
—a place where the fisherman was obliged to make his
offering of the first of his catch by taking two fishes
and placing them on the ku-ula stone as an offering to
Ku-ula.   Thus Aiai first put in practice the fishing
oblations established by his father at the place of his
birth, in his youth, but it was accomplished only
through the mana kupua of his parents.

When Aiai had finished calling on his parents and
instructing his friend, there were seen several persons
walking along the Haneoo beach with their fishing
baskets and setting them in the sea, but catching nothing.   At Aiai's suggestion he and his friend went over
to witness this fishing effort.   When they reached the
fishers Aiai asked them, "What are those things placed
there for ? "

They answered, "Those are baskets for catching
hinaleas, a fish that our King, Kamohoalii, longs for,
but we cannot get bait to catch the fish with."

"Why is it so? " asked Aiai.

And they answered, "Because Ku-ula and his family
are dead, and all the fish along the beach of Hana are
taken away."

Then Aiai asked them for two baskets.   Having
received them, he bade his friend take them and follow him.   They went to a little pool near the beach,
and setting the baskets therein, he called on his parents
for hinaleas.   As soon as he had finished, the fish

were seen coming in such numbers as to fill the pool, and still they came. Aiai now told his friend to go and fetch his parents and relatives to get fish, and to bring baskets with which to take home a supply; they should have the first pick, and the owners of the baskets should have the next chance. The messenger went with haste and brought his relatives as directed. Aiai then took two fishes and gave them to his friend to place on the ko'a they had established at Lehoula for the ku-ula. He also told him that before the setting of the sun of that day they would hear that King Kamohoalii of Hana was dead, choked and strangled to death by the fish. These prophetic words of Aiai came true.

After Aiai had made his offering, his friend's parents came to where the fish were gathering and were told to take all they desired, which they did, returning home happy for the liberal supply obtained without trouble. The owners of the baskets were then called and told to take all the fish they wished for themselves and for the King. When these people saw the great supply they were glad and much surprised at the success of these two boys. The news of the reappearing of the fish spread through the district, and the people flocked in great numbers and gathered hinaleas to their satisfaction, and returned to their homes with rejoicing. Some of those who gave Aiai the baskets returned with their bundles of fish to the King. When he saw so many of those he had longed for he became so excited that he reached out and picked one up and put it in his mouth, intending to eat it; but instead the fish slipped right into his throat and stuck there. Many tried to reach and take it out, but were unable, and before the sun set that day Kamohoalii, the King of Hana, died, being choked and strangled to death by the fish. Thus the words of Aiai, the son of Ku-ula, proved true.

By the death of the King of Hana the revenge was complete. The evil-doer from Molokai, and those who obeyed the King's orders on the day Ku-ula's house was fired, met retribution, and Aiai thus won a victory over all his father's enemies.

After living for a time at Hana Aiai left that place and went among the different islands of the group establishing fishing ko'as (*ko'a aina aumakua*). He was the first to measure the depth of the sea to locate these fishing ko'as for the deep sea fishermen who go out in their canoes, and the names of many of these ko'as located around the different islands are well known.

XXII

AIAI, SON OF KU-ULA

PART II OF THE LEGEND OF KU-ULA, THE FISH GOD OF HAWAII

TRANSLATED FROM MOKE MANU BY M. K. NAKUINA

AFTER the death of the King of Hana, Aiai left the people of Haneoo catching hinalea and went to Kumaka, a place where fresh water springs out from the sand and rocks near the surf of Puhele, at Hamoa, where lay a large, long stone in the sea. This stone he raised upright and also placed others about the water spring, and said to his friend: "To-day I name this stone Ku-a-lanakila, for I have triumphed over my enemies; and I hereby declare that all fishes, crabs, and sea-moss shall return again in plenty throughout the seas of Hana, as in the days when my parents were living in the flesh at Lehoula."

From the time Aiai raised this stone, up to the present generation, the story of Ku-ula and Aiai is well preserved, and people have flocked to the place where the stone stands to see it and verify the tradition. Some kahunas advise their suffering patients to pay a visit to the stone, Ku-lanakila, with some offerings for relief from their sickness and also to bathe in the spring of Kumaka and the surf of Puhele. This was a favorite spot of the kings and chiefs of the olden times for bathing and surf-riding, and is often referred to in the stories and legends of Hawaii-nei. This was the first stone raised by Aiai and established as a ku-ula at Hamoa; and the old people of Hana attributed to its influence the return of the fish to their waters.

After Aiai's practice of his father's instructions and the return of the fishes, his fame spread throughout the district, and the people made much of him during his stay with them.

A great service wrought by Aiai during his boyhood was the teaching of his friend and his friend's parents how to make the various nets for all kinds of fishing. He also taught them to make the different kinds of fishing lines. When they were skilled in all these branches of knowledge pertaining to fishing, he called the people together, and in their presence declared his friend to be the head fisherman of Hana, with full control of all the stations (*ko'a ia*) he had established. This wonder-working power second to none, possessed by Aiai, he now conferred on his friend, whereby his own name would be perpetuated and his fame established all over the land.

The first *ko'a ia* (fishing ground, or station) where Aiai measured the depth of the sea is near Aleamai, his birthplace, and is called Kapukaulua, where he hooked and killed the eel Koona. It is a few miles from the shore to the southeast of the rocky islet called Alau. The second station he established was at a spot about a mile from Haneoo and Hamoa which was for the kala, palani, nanue, puhi, and ula. These varieties of fish are not caught by nets, or with the hook, but in baskets which are filled with bait and let down in the deep sea.

The third station, which he named Koauli, was located out in the deep sea for the deep sea fishes, the depth ranging about two hundred fathoms. This is the ko'a that fishermen have to locate by certain shore bearings, lest a mistake be made as to the exact spot and the bottom be found rocky and the hooks entangle in the coral. In all the stations Aiai located there are no coral ledges where the fisherman's hook would catch, or the line be entangled; and old Hawaiians commended the skill of such locations, believing that the success of Aiai's work was due to his father's influence as an ocean deity.

At one time Aiai went over to the bay of Wananalua, the present port of Hana, with its noted hill of Kauiki and the sandy beach of Pueokahi. Here he made and placed a ku-ula, and also placed a fish stone in the cliff of Kauiki whereon is the ko'a known as Makakiloia. And the people of Hana give credit to this stone for the frequent appearance of the akule, oio, moi, and other fishes in their waters.

Aiai's good work did not stop at this point; proceeding to Honomaele he picked up three pebbles at the shore and, going into the sea, out beyond the breaking surf, he placed them there. In due time these three pebbles gathered others together and made a regular ridge; and when this was accomplished, the aweoweo gathered from the far ocean to this ridge of pebbles for rest; whereupon the people came with net, hook, and line, and caught them as they desired. The writer witnessed this in 1845 with his own eyes. This ko'a for aweoweo is still there, but difficult to locate, from the fact that all the old residents are gone—either dead or moved away.

He next went over to Waiohue, Koolau, where he placed a stone on a sharp rocky islet, called Paka, whereon a few puhala grow. It is claimed that during the season of the kala, they come in from the ocean, attracted to this locality by the power of this stone. They continue on to Mokumana, a cape between Keanae and Wailuanui. They come in gradually for two days, and on the third day of their reaching the coast, at the pali of Ohea, is the time and place to surround them with nets. In olden times while the fishermen were hauling in their nets full of kala into the canoes, the akule and oio also came in numbers at the same time, making it impossible to catch all in one day; and as there were so many gathered in the net it took them a day and a night before they could care for their draught, which yielded so many more than could be made use of that they were fed to the pigs and dogs. The kala of Ohea is noted for its fatness and fine flavor. Few people are now living there, and the people who knew all about this are dead; but the stone that Aiai placed on that little island at Waiohue is still there.

Aiai stayed there a few days and then returned to Hana and lived at his birthplace quite a length of time till he was a man grown. During this period he was teaching his art of fishing in all its forms; and when he was satisfied the people were proficient, he prepared to visit other places for like service. But before leaving, Aiai told his friend to go and kill the big *hee kupua* (wonderful octopus) in the deep sea, right out of Wailuanui, Koolau, and he consented.

When the canoes were made ready and drawn to the beach and the people came prepared to start, Aiai brought the *hokeo* (fishing gourd), where the *leho* (kauri shell) that Ku-ula his father gave him was kept, and gave it to his friend. This shell is called *lehoula*, and the locality at Hana of that name was called after it.

Then the canoes and people sailed away till they got out along the palis near Kopiliula, where they rested. Aiai was not with the party, but overlooked their operations from the pali of Puhiai. While they rested, preparation for the lowering of the leho was being made, and when ready, Aiai's friend called on Ku-ula and Hina for the assistance of their wonderful powers. When he was through, he took off the covering of the gourd and took out the leho, which had rich beautiful colors like the rainbow, and attaching it to the line, he lowered it into the sea, where it sent out rays of a fiery light. The hee was so attracted by its radiance that it came out of its hole and with its great arms, which were as long and large as a full-grown cocoanut tree, came up to the surface of the water and stood there like a cocoanut grove. The men were frightened, for it approached and went right into the canoes with the intention of destroying them and the men and capturing the leho; but it failed, because Aiai's friend, with his skill and power, had provided himself with a stone,

which, at the proper time, he shoved into the head of
the squid; and the weight of the stone drew it down
to the bottom of the sea and kept it there, and being
powerless to remove the stone, it died. The men
seized and cut off one of the arms, which was so big
that it loaded the canoes down so that they returned to
Hana. When the squid died, it turned to stone. It
is pointed out to-day just outside of Wailuanui, where
a stone formation resembles the body of a squid and
the arms, with one missing.

When Aiai saw from the pali that his friend was
successful in killing the hee, he returned to Hana
unseen, and in a short while the canoes arrived with its
arm, which was divided among the people according to
the directions of Aiai.

When Aiai saw that his friend and others of Hana
were skilled in all the art of fishing, he decided to
leave his birthplace and journey elsewhere. So he
called a council of his friends and told them of his
intended departure, to establish other fishing stations
and instruct the people with all the knowledge thereof
in conformity with the injunction of Ku-ula his father.
They approved of the course contemplated and
expressed their indebtedness to him for all the benefits
he had shown them.

On leaving Aleamai he took with him the fish-hook,
manaiaakalani, and the fish pearl, *Kahuoi*, for aku from
the little cave where he had lodged on the hill of
Kaiwiopele, and then disappeared in the mysterious
manner of his parents. He established ku-ulas and
ko'a aina, by placing three fish stones at various points

as far as Kipahulu. At the streams of Kikoo and Maulili there stands a stone to-day, which was thrown by Aiai and dropped at a bend in the waters, unmoved by the many freshets that have swept the valleys since that time.

Out in the sea of Maulili is a famous station known as Koanui. It is about a mile from the shore and marks the boundary of the sea of Maulili, and the fish that appear periodically and are caught within its limits have been subject to a division between the fishermen and the landowner ever since. This is a station where the fisherman's hook shall not return without a fish except the hook be lost, or the line cut.

The first time that Aiai tested this station and caught a fish with his noted hook, he saw a fisherman in his canoe drifting idly, without success. When he saw Aiai, this fisherman, called Kanemakua, paddled till he came close to where Aiai was floating on an improvised canoe, a wiliwili log, without an outrigger, —which much surprised him. Before the fisherman reached him, Aiai felt a tug at his line and knew that he had caught a fish and began pulling it in. When Kanemakua came within speaking distance Aiai greeted him and gave him the fish, putting it into his canoe. Kanemakua was made happy and thanked Aiai for his generosity. While putting it in the canoe Aiai said:

"This is the first time I have fished in these waters to locate (or found) this station, and as you are the first man I meet I give you the first fish caught. I also give you charge of this ko'a; but take my advice. When you come here to fish and see a man meeting you in a canoe and floating alongside of you, if at that time you have caught a fish, then give it to him as I have done to you, without regret, and thus get a good name and be known as a generous man. If you observe this, great benefits will come to you and those related to you."

As Aiai finished speaking he suddenly disappeared, and Kanemakua could hardly realize that he had not been dreaming but for the assurance he had in the great fish lying in his canoe. He returned to the shore with his prize, which was so large and heavy that it required the help of two others to carry it to the house, where it was cut up and the oven made hot for its baking. When it was cooked he took the eyes of the fish and offered them up as a thanksgiving sacrifice. Then the family, friends, and neighbors around came to the feast and ate freely. During all this time Kanemakua was thinking of the words spoken by the young man, which he duly observed. The first ku-ula established in Maulili, Maui, was named after him, and from that time its fish have been given out freely without restriction or division.

After establishing the different ku-ula stations along the coast from Hana to Kipahulu, Aiai went to Kaupo and other places. A noted station and ku-ula is at Kahikinui. All the stations of this place are in the deep sea, where they use nets of three kinds; there is also fishing with poles, and ulua fishing, because this part of the island faces the wind; but the ku-ulas are located on the seashore, as is also the one at Honuaula, where it is covered over by the lava flow.

Thus was performed the good work of Aiai in establishing ku-ula stations and fish stones all around the island of Maui. It is also said that he visited Kahoolawe and established a ku-ula at Hakioawa, though it differs from the others, being built on a high bluff overlooking the sea, somewhat like a temple, by placing stones in the form of a square, in the middle of which was left a space wherein the fishermen of that island laid their first fish caught, as a thank offering. Awa and kapa were also placed there as offerings to the fish deities.

An idea prevails with some people that the ko'a of Kamohoalii, the king shark of Kahoolawe, is on this island, but if all the stories told of it be examined there will be found no reference to a ko'a of his on this island.

From Kahoolawe, Aiai next went to Lanai, where he started fishing for *aku* (bonito) at Cape Kaunolu, using his pearl Kahuoi. This is the first case known of fishing for aku with pearl from the land, as it is a well known fact that this fish is caught only in deep sea, far from shore. In the story of Kaneapua it is shown that he is the only one who had fished for aku at the Cape of Kaunolu, where it was started by Aiai.

From Kaunolu, Aiai went to Kaena Cape, where at a place close to Paomai, was a little sandy beach now known as Polihua. Here he took a stone and carved a figure on it, then carried and placed it on the sandy beach, and called on his parents. While making his incantations the stone moved toward the sea and disappeared under the water. His incantations finished, the stone reappeared and moved toward him till it reached the place where it had been laid; whereupon it was transformed into a turtle, and gave the name of Polihua to that beach. This work of Aiai on the island of Lanai was the first introduction of the turtle in the seas of Hawaii, and also originated the habit of the turtle of going up the beach to lay its eggs, then returning to the sea.

After making the circuit of Lanai he went over to Molokai, landing at Punakou and travelled along the shore till he reached Kaunakakai. At this place he saw spawns of mullet, called Puai-i, right near the shore, which he kicked with his foot, landing them on the sand. This practice of kicking fish with the feet is carried on to this time, but only at that locality. Aiai continued on along the Kona side of Molokai, examining its fishing grounds and establishing ku-ulas till he got to Halawa. At the Koolau side of the island he stopped at Wailau and saw the cave of the eel Koona that went to Hana and stole the fish from his father's pond, and the cause of all the trouble that befell his parents and himself.

When Aiai landed at Wailau he saw that both sides of the valley were covered with men, women, and children engaged in closing up the stream and diverting its water to another course, whereby they would be enabled to catch oopu and opae. The water being low, the gourds of some of the people were full from their catch.

Aiai noticed their wanton method of fishing, whereby all oopus and opaes were caught without thought of any reservation for their propagation; therefore he called on his parents to take them all away. The prayer was granted, for suddenly they all disappeared; those in the water went up the stream to a place called Koki, while those in the gourds were turned to lizards which scampered out and ran all over the rocks. The people were much surprised at this change and felt sorely disappointed at the loss of their food supply.

On account of his regard for a certain lad of that place, named Kahiwa, he showed him the place of the opaes to be up the precipitous cliff, Koki. The youth was attentive to the direction of Aiai and going there he found the oopus and opaes as stated, as they are to this day. That is what established the noted saying of the old people of that land: "Kokio of Wailau is the ladder of the opae." It is also known as the "Pali of Kahiwa."

When Aiai left Wailau he showed this lad the ku-ula and the fish station in the sea he had located there, at the same distance as that rocky island known as Mokapu. He went also to Pelekunu, Waikolu and Kalawao, even to Kalaupapa, the present home of the lepers. At the latter place he left a certain fish stone. That is the reason fish constantly gather there even to this day. He also went to Hoolehua and so on as far as *Ka lae o ka ilio* (the dog's forehead) and *Ka lae o ka laau*. Between these two capes in the sea is a station established by Aiai, where a tree grew out from under a rock, Ekaha by name. It is a hardwood tree, but the trunk and also the branches are without leaves.   This place is a great haunt for fishermen with their hooks.

Aiai then came to Oahu, first landing at Makapuu, in Koolau, where he founded a *pohaku-ia* (fish stone) for red fish and for speckled fish, and called it Malei. This was a female rock, and the fish of that place is the uhu.   It is referred to in the mele of Hiiaka, thus:

> " I will not go to the stormy capes of Koolau,
>   The sea-cliffs of Moeaau.
>   The woman watching uhu of Makapuu
>   Dwells on the ledge of Kamakani
>   At Koolau.   The living
>   Offers grass-twined sacrifices, O Malie ! "

From the time Aiai founded that spawning-place until the present, its fish have been the uhu, extending to Hanauma.   There were also several gathering-places for fish established outside of Kawaihoa.   Aiai next moved to Maunalua, then to Waialae and Kahalaia.   At Kaalawai he placed a white and brown rock.   There in that place is a hole filled with aholehole, therefore the name of the land is Kaluahole. Right outside of Kahuahui there is a station where Aiai placed a large round sandstone that is surrounded by spawning-places for fish; Ponahakeone is its name.

In ancient times the chiefs selected a very secret place wherein to hide the dead bodies of their greatly beloved, lest some one should steal their bones to make fish-hooks, or arrows to shoot mice with.   For that reason the ancients referred to Ponahakeone as "*He Lualoa no Na'lii*"—a deep pit for the chiefs.

Aiai came to Kalia and so on to Kakaako. Here he was befriended by a man named Apua, with whom he remained several days, observing and listening to the murmurs of the chief named Kou. This chief was a skilful hiaku fisherman, his grounds being outside of Mamala until you came to Moanalua. There was none so skilled as he, and generous withal, giving akus to the people throughout the district.

As Aiai was dwelling with his friend Apua at Kakaako, he meandered off one day along the shore of Kulolia, and so on to Pakaka and Kapapoko. But he did not return to the house of his friend, for he met a young woman gathering *limu* (sea-moss) and fishing for crabs. This young woman, whose name was Puiwa, lived at Hanakaialama and was a virgin, never having had a husband. She herself, as the people would say, was forward to ask Aiai to be her husband; but he listened to her voice, and they went up together to her home and saw the parents and relatives, and forthwith were married. After living with this young woman some time a son was born to them, whom Aiai named Puniaiki. During those days was the distribution of aku which were sent up from Honolulu to the different dwellings; but while others were given a whole fish, they got but a portion from some neighbor. For this reason the woman was angry, and told Aiai to go to the brook and get some oopus fit to eat, as well as opae. Aiai listened to the voice of his wife. He dug a ditch and constructed a dam so as to lead the water of the brook into some pits, and thus be able to catch the oopu and opae. He labored some days at this work, and the fish and shrimps were hung up to dry.

On a certain day following, Aiai and his wife went with their child to the brook. She left her son upon the bank of the stream while she engaged herself in catching opae and oopu from the pits. But it was not long before the child began to cry; and as he cried, Aiai told his wife to leave her fishing, but she talked saucily to him. So Aiai called upon the names of his ancestors. Immediately a dark and lowering cloud drew near and poured out a flood of water upon the stream, and in a short time the dam was broken by the freshet and all the oopu and opae, together with the child, were swept toward the sea. But the woman was not taken by the flood. Aiai then rose up and departed, without thought of his wife.

He went down from the valley to Kaumakapili, and as he was standing there he saw some women fishing for oopu on the banks of the stream, the daughter of the chief Kikihale being with them. At that time, behold, there was caught by the female guardian of the daughter of Kikihale a very large oopu. This oopu she showed to her *protégée*, who told her to put it into a large calabash with water and feed it with limu, so that it might become a pet fish. This was done and the oopu was tended very carefully night and day.

Aiai stood by and saw the fish lifted out of the brook, and recognized it at the same time as his own child, changed from a human being into an oopu.

(At this point the story of Aiai gives place to that of his child.)

When the oopu was placed in a large calabash with water, it was carefully tended and fed with sea-moss for some time, but one day in seeing to this duty the guardian of the chiefess, on reaching the calabash, was startled to behold therein a human child, looking with its eyes. And the water in the calabash had disappeared. She was greatly surprised and seized with a dark foreboding, and a trembling fear possessed her as she looked upon this miraculous child.

This woman went and told the chiefess of this child they knew to have had the form of an oopu, and as Kikihale heard the story of her guardian she went quickly, with grave doubts, however, of this her report; but there, on reaching the calabash, as she looked she saw indeed a child therein. She immediately put forth her hands toward the child and lifting it, carefully examined its form and noted its agreeable features. As the thought quickly possessed this girl, she said: "Now, my guardian, you and your husband take and rear this child till he is grown, then I will be his wife."

The guardian answered her: "When this child becomes grown you will be old; that is, your days will be in the evening of life, while his place will be in the early morn. Will you not thereby have lasting cause for dissatisfaction and contention between you in the future?"

Kikihale answering her guardian said: "You are not to blame; these things are mine to consider, for the reason that the desire is mine, not yours, my guardian."

After this talking the child was quickly known of among the chiefs and attendants. He was nourished and brought up to adult age, when Kikihale took him for her husband as she had said; and for a time they dwelt together as man and wife without disagreement between them. But during these days Kikihale saw plainly that her husband was not disposed to do anything for their support; therefore she mourned over it continually and angrily reproved him, finally, saying:

"O my husband, can you not go forth also, as others, to assist our father and the attendants in the duties of fishing, instead of eating till you are satisfied, then rolling over with face upward to the ridge-pole of the house and counting the ahos? It may do while my father is alive; but if he should die, whence would come our support?" Thus she spoke reproachingly from day to day, and the words stung Puniaiki's heart with much pain.

And this is what he said to his wife one day: "It is unpleasant to hear you constantly talking thus. Not as wild animals is the catching of fish in the sea; they are obedient if called, and you may eat wastefully of my fish when procured. I have authority over fish, men, pigs, and dogs. If you are a favorite of your father then go to him for double canoes, with their fishing appurtenances, and men to paddle them."

When Kikihale heard these words of her husband she hastened to Kou, her father, and told him all that Puniaiki had said, and the request was promptly executed. Kikihale returned to her husband and told him all she had done.

On Puniaiki's going down to the canoe place he found the men were making ready the canoes with the nets, rods, lines, and the pearl fish-hooks. Here he lit a fire and burned up the pearl fish-hooks, at which his wife was much angered and cried loudly for the hiaku pearl hooks of her father. She went and told Kou of this mischievous action of her husband, but he answered her not a word at this act of his son-in-law, though he had supplied five gourds filled with them, a thousand in number, and the strangest thing was, that all were burned up save two only which Kou had reserved.

That night Puniaiki slept apart from his wife, and he told the canoe paddlers to sleep in the canoe sheds, not to go to their homes that night; and they obeyed his voice.

It was Kou's habit to rouse his men before break of day to sail in the malaus for aku fishing at the mouth of the harbor, for that was their feeding-time, not after the sun had risen. Thus would the canoes enter the schools of aku and this chief became famous thereby as a most successful fisherman. But on this day was seen the sorcerer's work of this child of Aiai.

As Kou with his men set out always before dawn, here was this Puniaiki above at his place at sunrise. At this time on his awaking from sleep he turned his face mountainward, and looking at Kaumakapili he saw a rainbow and its reddish mist spread out at that place, wherein was standing a human form. He felt conscious that it was Aiai his father, therefore he went there and Aiai showed him the place of the *pa* (fish-hook) called Kahuai, and he said to his son: "Here will I stay till you return; be quick."

Upon Puniaiki reaching the landing the canoes were quickly made ready to depart, and as they reached Kapapoko and Pakaka, at the sea of Kuloloia, they went on to Ulukua, now the lighthouse location of Honolulu harbor. At this place Puniaiki asked the paddlers: "What is the name of that surf cresting beneath the prow of our canoes?"

"Puuiki," replied the men.

He then said to them: "Point straight the prow of the canoes and paddle with strength." At these words of Puniaiki their minds were in doubt, because there were probably no akus at that place in the surf; but that was none of their business. As they neared the breakers of Puuiki, below the mouth of Mamala, Puniaiki said to his men: "Turn the canoes around and go shorewards." And in returning he said quickly, "Paddle strong, for here we are on the top of a school of akus." But strange to say, as the men looked in the water they saw no fish swimming about, but on reaching Ulakua Puniaiki opened up the fish-hook, Kahuai, from its wrapping in the gourd and held it in his hand.

At this the akus, unprecedented in number, fairly leaped into the canoes. They became so filled with the fish, without labor, that they sank in the water as they reached Kapuukolo, and the men jumped overboard to float them to the beach. The canoe men

wondered greatly at this work of the son-in-law of
Kou the chief; and the shore people shouted as the
akus which filled the harbor swam toward the fish-
pond of Kuwili and on to the mouth of Leleo stream.

When the canoes touched shore Puniaiki seized
two fishes in his hands and went to join his father
where he was staying, and Aiai directed him to take
them up to where his mother lived. These akus
were not gifts for her, but an offering to Ku-ula at a
ko'a established just above Kahuailanawai. Puniaiki
obeyed the instructions of his father, and on returning
to him he was sent back to his mother, Puiwa, with a
supply of akus. She was greatly surprised that this
handsome young man, with his gift of akus for her to
eat, was her own son, and these were the first fruits of
his labor.

The people marvelled at the quantity of fish
throughout the harbor, so that even the stream at
Kikihale was also full of akus, and Puniaiki commanded the people to take of them day and night;
and the news of this visit of akus went all around
Oahu. This unequalled haul of akus was a great
humiliation to Kou, affecting his fame as a fisherman;
but he was neither jealous of his son-in-law nor angry,
—he just sat silent. He thought much on the subject but with kindly feelings, resulting in turning over
this employment to him who could prosecute it without worry.

Shortly afterwards Aiai arranged with Puniaiki for
the establishing of ku-ulas, ko'as, and fish stones
around the island of Oahu, which were as follows:

The Kou stone was for Honolulu and Kaumakapili; a ku-ula at Kupahu; a fish stone at Hanapouli, Ewa. Ahuena was the ku-ula for Waipio; two were assigned for Honouliuli. Hani-o was the name of the ko'a outside of Kalaeloa; Kua and Maunalahilahi for Waianae; Kamalino for Waimea; and Kaihukuuna for Laiemaloo, Koolau.

Aiai and his son also visited Kauai and Niihau on this work, then they turned and went together to Hawaii. The principal or most noted fishing-grounds there are: Poo-a, Kahaka, and Olelomoana at Kona; Kalae at Kau; Kupakea at Puna, and I at Hilo.

In former times at most of these fishing-grounds were seen multitudes and varieties of fish, all around the islands, and occasionally deep sea kinds came close in shore, but in this new era there are not so many. Some people say it is on account of the change of the times.

XXIII

KANEAUKAI

A LEGEND OF WAIALUA

THOS. G. THRUM

L ONG ago, when the Hawaiians were in the darkness of superstition and kahunaism, with their gods and lords many, there lived at Mokuleia, Waialua, two old men whose business it was to pray to Kaneaukai for a plentiful supply of fish. These men were quite poor in worldly possessions, but given to the habit of drinking a potion of awa after their evening meal of poi and fish.

The fish that frequented the waters of Mokuleia were the aweoweo, kala, manini, and many other varieties that find their habitat inside the coral reefs. Crabs of the white variety burrowed in the sand near the seashore and were dug out by the people, young and old. The squid also were speared by the skilful fishermen, and were eaten stewed, or salted and sun-dried and roasted on the coals. The salt likely came from Kaena Point, from salt-water evaporation in the holes of rocks so plentiful on that stormy cape. Or it may have been made on the salt pans of Paukauwila, near the stream of that name, where a few years ago this industry existed on a small scale.

But to return to our worshippers of Kaneaukai. One morning on going out upon the seashore they found a log of wood, somewhat resembling the human form, which they took home and set in a corner of their lowly hut, and continued their habit of praying to Kaneaukai. One evening, after having prepared a scanty supper of poi and salt, with perhaps a few roasted kukui-nuts, as a relish, and a couple of cocoanut cups of awa as their usual drink, they saw a handsome young man approaching, who entered their hut and saluted them. He introduced himself by saying, "I am Kaneaukai to whom you have been praying, and that which you have set up is my image; you have done well in caring for it."

He sat down, after the Hawaiian custom, as if to share their evening meal, which the two old men invited him to partake of with them, but regretted the scanty supply of awa. He said: "Pour the awa back into the bowl and divide into three." This they did and at once shared their meal with their guest.

After supper Kaneaukai said to the two old men, "Go to Keawanui and you will get fish enough for the present." He then disappeared, and the fishermen went as instructed and obtained three fishes; one they gave to an old sorceress who lived near by, and the other two they kept for themselves.

Soon after this there was a large school of fish secured by the fishermen of Mokuleia. So abundant were the fish that after salting all they could, there was enough to give away to the neighbors; and even the dogs had more than they desired.

Leaving the Mokuleia people to the enjoyment of their unusual supply of fish, we will turn to the abode of two kahunas, who were also fishermen, living on the south side of Waimea Valley, Oahu. One morning, being out of fish, they went out into the harbor to try their luck, and casting their net they caught up a calcareous stone about as large as a man's head, and a pilot fish. They let the pilot fish go, and threw the stone back into the sea. Again they cast their net and again they caught the stone and the pilot fish; and so again at the third haul. At this they concluded that the stone was a representative of some god. The elder of the two said: "Let us take this stone ashore and set it up as an idol, but the pilot fish we will let go." So they did, setting it up on the turn of the bluff on the south side of the harbor of Waimea. They built an inclosure about it and smoothed off the rocky bluff by putting flat stones from the immediate neighborhood about the stone idol thus strangely found.

About ten days after the finding of the stone idol the two old kahunas were sitting by their grass hut in the dusk of the evening, bewailing the scarcity of fish, when Kaneaukai himself appeared before them in the guise of a young man. He told them that they had done well in setting up his stone image, and if they would follow his directions they would have a plentiful supply of fish. Said he, "Go to Mokuleia, and you will find my wooden idol; bring it here and set it up alongside of my stone idol." But they demurred, as it was a dark night and there were usually quicksands after a freshet in the Kamananui River. His answer was, "Send your grandsons." And so the two young men were sent to get the wooden idol and were told where they could find it.

The young men started for Mokuleia by way of Kaika, near the place where salt was made a few years ago. Being strangers, they were in doubt about the true way, when a meteor (*hoku kaolele*) appeared and went before them, showing them how to escape the quicksands. After crossing the river they went on to Mokuleia as directed by Kaneaukai, and found the wooden idol in the hut of the two old men. They shouldered it, and taking as much dried fish as they could carry, returned by the same way that they had come, arriving at home about midnight.

The next day the two old kahunas set up the wooden idol in the same inclosure with the stone representative of Kaneaukai. The wooden image has long since disappeared, having been destroyed, probably, at the time Kaahumanu made a tour of Oahu after her conversion to Christianity, when she issued her edict to burn all the idols. But the stone idol was not destroyed. Even during the past sixty years offerings of roast pigs are known to have been placed before it. This was done secretly for fear of the chiefs, who had published laws against idolatry.

Accounts differ, various narrators giving the story some embellishments of their own. So good a man as a deacon of Waialua in telling the above seemed to believe that, instead of being a legend it was true; for an old man, to whom he referred as authority, said that one of the young men who went to Mokuleia and brought the wooden idol to Waimea was his own grandfather.

An aged resident of the locality gives this version: Following the placement of their strangely found stone these two men dreamed of Kaneaukai as a god in some far-distant land, to whom they petitioned that he would crown their labors with success by granting them a plentiful supply of fish. Dreaming thus, Kaneaukai revealed himself to them as being already at their shore; that the stone which they had been permitted to find and had honored by setting up at Kehauapuu, was himself, in response to their petitions; and since they had been faithful so far, upon continuance of the same, and offerings thereto, they should ever after be successful in their fishing. As if in confirmation of this covenant, this locality has ever since been noted for the periodical visits of schools of the anae-holo and kala, which are prevalent from April to July, coming, it is said, from Ohea, Honuaula, Maui, by way of Kahuku, and returning the same way.

So strong was the superstitious belief of the people in this deified stone that when, some twenty years ago, the road supervisor of the district threw it over and broke off a portion, it was prophesied that Kaneaukai would be avenged for the insult. And when shortly afterward the supervisor lost his position and removed from the district, returning not to the day of his death; and since several of his relatives have met untimely ends, not a few felt it was the recompense of his sacrilegious act.

XXIV

THE SHARK-MAN, NANAUE

MRS. E. M. NAKUINA

KAMOHOALII, the King-shark of Hawaii and Maui, has several deep sea caves that he uses in turn as his habitat. There are several of these at the bottom of the palisades, extending from Waipio toward Kohala, on the island of Hawaii. A favorite one was at Koamano, on the mainland, and another was at Maiaukiu, the small islet just abreast of the valley of Waipio. It was the belief of the ancient Hawaiians that several of these shark gods could assume any shape they chose, the human form even, when occasion demanded.

In the reign of Umi, a beautiful girl, called Kalei, living in Waipio, was very fond of shellfish, and frequently went to Kuiopihi for her favorite article of diet. She generally went in the company of other women, but if the sea was a little rough, and her usual companion was afraid to venture out on the wild and dangerous beach, she very often went alone rather than go without her favorite sea-shells.

In those days the Waipio River emptied over a low fall into a basin partly open to the sea; this basin is now completely filled up with rocks from some convulsion of nature, which has happened since then. In this was a deep pool, a favorite bathing-place for all Waipio. The King shark god, Kamohoalii, used to visit this pool very often to sport in the fresh waters of the Waipio River. Taking into account the many different tales told of the doings of this shark god, he must have had quite an eye for human physical beauty.

Kalei, as was to be expected from a strong, well-formed Hawaiian girl of those days, was an expert swimmer, a good diver, and noted for the neatness and grace with which she would *lelekawa* (jump from the rocks into deep water) without any splashing of water, which would happen to unskilful divers, from the awkward attitudes they would assume in the act of jumping.

It seems Kamohoalii, the King-shark, had noted the charms of the beautiful Kalei, and his heart, or whatever answers in place of it with fishes, had been captured by them. But he could not expect to make much of an impression on the maiden's susceptibilities *in propria persona*, even though he was perfectly able to take her bodily into his capacious maw; so he must needs go courting in a more pleasing way. Assuming the form of a very handsome man, he walked on the beach one rather rough morning, waiting for the girl's appearance.

Now the very wildness of the elements afforded him the chance he desired, as, though Kalei was counted among the most agile and quick of rock-fishers, that morning, when she did come, and alone, as her usual companions were deterred by the rough weather, she made several unsuccessful springs to escape a high threatening wave raised by the god himself; and apparently, if it had not been for the prompt and effective assistance rendered by the handsome stranger, she would have been swept out into the sea.

Thus an acquaintance was established. Kalei met the stranger from time to time, and finally became his wife.

Some little time before she expected to become a mother, her husband, who all this time would only come home at night, told her his true nature, and informing her that he would have to leave her, gave orders in regard to the bringing up of the future child. He particularly cautioned the mother never to let him be fed on animal flesh of any kind, as he would be born with a dual nature, and with a body that he could change at will.

In time Kalei was delivered of a fine healthy boy, apparently the same as any other child, but he had, besides the normal mouth of a human being, a shark's mouth on his back between the shoulder blades. Kalei had told her family of the kind of being her husband was, and they all agreed to keep the matter of the shark-mouth on the child's back a secret, as there was no knowing what fears and jealousies might be excited in the minds of the King or high chiefs by such an abnormal being, and the babe might be killed.

The old grandfather, far from heeding the warning given by Kamohoalii in the matter of animal diet, as soon as the boy, who was called Nanaue, was old enough to come under the taboo in regard to the eat-

ing of males, and had to take his meals at the mua
house with the men of the family, took especial pains
to feed him on dog meat and pork. He had a hope
that his grandson would grow up to be a great, strong
man, and become a famous warrior; and there was no
knowing what possibilities lay before a strong, skilful
warrior in those days. So he fed the boy with meat,
whenever it was obtainable. The boy thrived, grew
strong, big, and handsome as a young lama (*Maba
sandwicensis*) tree.

There was another pool with a small fall of the
Waipio River very near the house of Kalei, and the
boy very often went into it while his mother watched
on the banks. Whenever he got into the water he
would take the form of a shark and would chase and
eat the small fish which abounded in the pool. As he
grew old enough to understand, his mother took
especial pains to impress on him the necessity of con-
cealing his shark nature from other people.

This place was also another favorite bathing-place
of the people, but Nanaue, contrary to all the habits
of a genuine Hawaiian, would never go in bathing
with the others, but always alone; and when his
mother was able, she used to go with him and sit on
the banks, holding the kapa scarf, which he always
wore to hide the shark-mouth on his back.

When he became a man, his appetite for animal
diet, indulged in childhood, had grown so strong that
a human being's ordinary allowance would not suffice
for him. The old grandfather had died in the meantime, so that he was dependent on the food supplied

by his stepfather and uncles, and they had to expostulate with him on what they called his shark-like voracity. This gave rise to the common native nickname of a *manohae* (ravenous shark) for a very gluttonous man, especially in the matter of meat.

Nanaue used to spend a good deal of his time in the two pools, the one inland and the other opening into the sea. The busy-bodies (they had some in those days as well as now) were set to wondering why he always kept a *kihei*, or mantle, on his shoulders; and for such a handsomely shaped, athletic young man, it was indeed a matter of wonder and speculation, considering the usual attire of the youth of those days. He also kept aloof from all the games and pastimes of the young people, for fear that the wind or some active movement might displace the kapa mantle, and the shark-mouth be exposed to view.

About this time children and eventually grown-up people began to disappear mysteriously.

Nanaue had one good quality that seemed to redeem his apparent unsociability; he was almost always to be seen working in his mother's taro or potato patch when not fishing or bathing. People going to the sea beach would have to pass these potato or taro patches, and it was Nanaue's habit to accost them with the query of where they were going. If they answered, "To bathe in the sea," or, "Fishing," he would answer, "Take care, or you may disappear head and tail." Whenever he so accosted any one it would not be long before some member of the party so addressed would be bitten by a shark.

If it should be a man or woman going to the beach
alone, that person would never be seen again, as the
shark-man would immediately follow, and watching for
a favorable opportunity, jump into the sea. Having
previously marked the whereabouts of the person he
was after, it was an easy thing for him to approach
quite close, and changing into a shark, rush on the
unsuspecting person and drag him or her down into
the deep, where he would devour his victim at his
leisure. This was the danger to humanity which his
king-father foresaw when he cautioned the mother of
the unborn child about feeding him on animal flesh, as
thereby an appetite would be evoked which they had
no means of satisfying, and a human being would
furnish the most handy meal of the kind that he
would desire.

Nanaue had been a man grown some time, when an
order was promulgated by Umi, King of Hawaii, for
every man dwelling in Waipio to go to *koele* work,
tilling a large plantation for the King. There were to
be certain days in an *anahulu* (ten days) to be set aside
for this work, when every man, woman, and child had
to go and render service, excepting the very old and
decrepit, and children in arms.

The first day every one went but Nanaue. He kept
on working in his mother's vegetable garden to the
astonishment of all who saw him. This was reported
to the King, and several stalwart men were sent after
him. When brought before the King he still wore his
kapa kihei, or mantle.

The King asked him why he was not doing koele

work with every one else. Nanaue answered he did not know it was required of him. Umi could not help admiring the bold, free bearing of the handsome man, and noting his splendid physique, thought he would make a good warrior, greatly wanted in those ages, and more especially in the reign of Umi, and simply ordered him to go to work.

Nanaue obeyed, and took his place in the field with the others, and proved himself a good worker, but still kept on his kihei, which it would be natural to suppose that he would lay aside as an incumbrance when engaged in hard labor. At last some of the more venturesome of the younger folks managed to tear his kapa off, as if accidentally, when the shark-mouth on his back was seen by all the people near.

Nanaue was so enraged at the displacement of his kapa and his consequent exposure, that he turned and bit several of the crowd, while the shark-mouth opened and shut with a snap, and a clicking sound was heard such as a shark is supposed to make when baulked by its prey.

The news of the shark-mouth and his characteristic shark-like actions were quickly reported to the King, with the fact of the disappearance of so many people in the vicinity of the pools frequented by Nanaue; and of his pretended warnings to people going to the sea, which were immediately followed by a shark bite or by their being eaten bodily, with every one's surmise and belief that this man was at the bottom of all those disappearances. The King believed it was even so, and ordered a large fire to be lighted, and Nanaue to be thrown in to be burnt alive.

When Nanaue saw what was before him, he called on the shark god, his father, to help him; then, seeming to be endowed with superhuman strength in answer to his prayer, he burst the ropes with which he had been bound in preparation for the burning, and breaking through the throng of Umi's warriors, who attempted to detain him, he ran, followed by the whole multitude, toward the pool that emptied into the sea. When he got to the edge of the rocks bordering the pool, he waited till the foremost persons were within arm's length, when he leaped into the water and immediately turned into a large shark on the surface of the water, in plain view of the people who had arrived, and whose numbers were being continually augmented by more and more arrivals.

He lay on the surface some little time, as if to recover his breath, and then turned over on his back, and raising his head partly out of the water, snapped his teeth at the crowd who, by this time, completely lined the banks, and then, as if in derision or defiance of them, turned and flirted his tail at them and swam out to sea.

The people and chiefs were for killing his mother and relatives for having brought up such a monster. Kalei and her brothers were seized, bound, and dragged before Umi, while the people clamored for their immediate execution, or as some suggested, that they be thrown into the fire lighted for Nanaue.

But Umi was a wise king and would not consent to

any such summary proceedings, but questioned Kalei in regard to her fearful offspring. The grieved and frightened mother told everything in connection with the paternity and bringing up of the child, and with the warning given by the dread sea-father.

Umi considered that the great sea god Kamohoalii was on the whole a beneficent as well as a powerful one. Should the relatives and mother of that shark god's son be killed, there would then be no possible means of checking the ravages of that son, who might linger around the coast and creeks of the island, taking on human shape at will, for the purpose of travelling inland to any place he liked, and then reassume his fish form and lie in wait in the many deep pools formed by the streams and springs.

Umi, therefore, ordered Kalei and her relatives to be set at liberty, while the priests and shark kahunas were requested to make offerings and invocations to Kamohoalii that his spirit might take possession of one of his *hakas* (mediums devoted to his cult), and so express to humanity his desires in regard to his bad son, who had presumed to eat human beings, a practice well known to be contrary to Kamohoalii's design.

This was done, whereupon the shark god manifested himself through a haka, and expressed his grief at the action of his wayward son. He told them that the grandfather was to blame for feeding him on animal flesh contrary to his orders, and if it were not for that extenuating circumstance, he would order his son to be killed by his own shark officers; but as it was, he would require of him that he should disappear forever from the shores of Hawaii. Should Nanaue disregard that order and be seen by any of his father's shark soldiers, he was to be instantly killed.

Then the shark god, who it seems retained an affection for his human wife, exacted a promise that she and her relatives were to be forever free from any persecutions on account of her unnatural son, on pain of the return and freedom from the taboo of that son.

Accordingly Nanaue left the island of Hawaii, crossed over to Maui, and landing at Kipahulu, resumed his human shape and went inland. He was seen by the people, and when questioned, told them he was a traveller from Hawaii, who had landed at Hana and was going around sightseeing. He was so good looking, pleasant, and beguiling in his conversation that people generally liked him. He was taken as *aikane* by one of the petty chiefs of the place, who gave his own sister for wife to Nanaue. The latter made a stipulation that his sleeping house should be separated from that of his wife, on account of a pretended vow, but really in order that his peculiar second mouth might escape detection.

For a while the charms of the pretty girl who had become his wife seem to have been sufficient to prevent him from trying to eat human beings, but after a while, when the novelty of his position as a husband had worn off, and the desire for human flesh had again become very strong, he resumed the old practice for which he had been driven away from Hawaii.

He was eventually detected in the very act of pushing a girl into the sea, jumping in after her, then turning into a shark, and commencing to devour her, to the horror of some people who were fishing with hook and rod from some rocks where he had not observed them. These people raised the alarm, and Nanaue seeing that he was discovered, left for Molokai where he was not known.

He took up his residence on Molokai at Poniuohua, adjoining the ahupuaa of Kainalu, and it was not very long before he was at his old practice of observing and accosting people, giving them his peculiar warning, following them to the sea in his human shape, then seizing one of them as a shark and pulling the unfortunate one to the bottom, where he would devour his victim. In the excitement of such an occurrence, people would fail to notice his absence until he would reappear at some distant point far away from the throng, as if engaged in shrimping or crabbing.

This went on for some time, till the frightened and harassed people in desperation went to consult a shark kahuna, as the ravages of the man-eating shark had put a practical taboo on all kinds of fishing. It was not safe to be anywhere near the sea, even in the shallowest water.

The kahuna told them to lie in wait for Nanaue, and the next time he prophesied that a person would be eaten head and tail, to have some strong men seize him and pull off his kapa mantle, when a shark mouth would be found on his back. This was done, and the mouth seen, but the shark-man was so strong when they seized him and attempted to bind him, that he

broke away from them several times. He was finally
overpowered near the seashore and tightly bound. All
the people then turned their attention to gathering
brush and firewood to burn him, for it was well known
that it is only by being totally consumed by fire that
a man-shark can be thoroughly destroyed, and
prevented from taking possession of the body of some
harmless fish shark, who would then be incited to do
all the pernicious acts of a man-shark.

While he lay there on the low sandy beach, the tide
was coming in, and as most of the people were returning with fagots and brush, Nanaue made a supreme
effort and rolled over so that his feet touched the
water, when he was enabled at once to change into a
monster shark. Those who were near him saw it, but
were not disposed to let him off so easily, and they ran
several rows of netting makai, the water being very
shallow for quite a distance out. The shark's flippers
were all bound by the ropes with which the man
Nanaue had been bound, and this with the shallowness
of the water prevented him from exerting his great
strength to advantage. He did succeed in struggling
to the breakers, though momentarily growing weaker
from loss of blood, as the people were striking at him
with clubs, spears, stone adzes and anything that
would hurt or wound, so as to prevent his escape.

With all that, he would have got clear, if the people
had not called to their aid the demigod Unauna, who
lived in the mountains of upper Kainalu. It was then
a case of Akua vs. Akua, but Unauna was only a
young demigod, and not supposed to have acquired

his full strength and supernatural powers, while Nanaue was a full-grown man and shark. If it had not been for the latter's being hampered by the cords with which he was bound, the nets in his way, as well as the loss of blood, it is fully believed that he would have got the better of the young local presiding deity; but he was finally conquered and hauled up on the hill slopes of Kainalu to be burnt.

The shallow ravine left by the passage of his immense body over the light yielding soil of the Kainalu Hill slope can be seen to this day, as also a ring or deep groove completely around the top of a tall insulated rock very near the top of Kainalu Hill, around which Unauna had thrown the rope, to assist him in hauling the big shark uphill. The place was ever afterwards called Puumano (Shark Hill), and is so known to this day.

Nanaue was so large, that in the attempt to burn him, the blood and water oozing out of his burning body put out the fire several times. Not to be out-witted in that way by the shark son of Kamohoalii, Unauna ordered the people to cut and bring for the purpose of splitting into knives, bamboos from the sacred grove of Kainalu. The shark flesh was then cut into strips, partly dried, and then burnt, but the whole bamboo grove had to be used before the big shark was all cut. The god Mohoalii (another form of the name of the god Kamohoalii), father of Unauna, was so angered by the desecration of the grove, or more likely on account of the use to which it was put, that he took away all the edge and sharpness from the bamboos of this grove forever, and to this day they are different from the bamboos of any other place or grove on the islands, in this particular, that a piece of them cannot cut any more than any piece of common wood.

XXV

FISH STORIES AND SUPERSTITIONS

TRANSLATED BY M. K. NAKUINA

THE following narration of the different fishes
here given is told and largely believed in by
native fishermen. All may not agree as to particulars
in this version, but the main features are well known
and vary but little. Some of these stories are termed
mythical, in others the truth is never questioned, and
together they have a deep hold on the Hawaiian mind.
Further and confirmatory information may be obtained
from fishermen and others, and by visiting the market
the varieties here mentioned may be seen almost daily.

In the olden time certain varieties of fish were
tabooed and could not be caught at all times, being
subject to the kapu of Ku-ula, the fish god, who
propagated the finny tribes of Hawaiian waters.
While deep sea fishing was more general, that in the
shallow sea, or along shore, was subject to the restric-
tions of the konohiki of the land, and aliis, both as to
certain kinds and periods. The sign of the shallow
sea kapu was the placing of branches of the hau tree
all along the shore. The people seeing this token of
the kapu respected it, and any violation thereof in
ancient times was said to be punishable by death.

While this kapu prevailed the people resorted to the deep sea stations for their food supply. With the removal of the hau branches, indicating that the kapu was lifted, the people fished as they desired, subject only to the makahiki taboo days of the priest or alii, when no canoes were allowed to go out upon the water.

The first fish caught by a fisherman, or any one else, was marked and dedicated to Ku-ula. After this offering was made, Ku-ula's right therein being thus recognized, they were free from further oblations so far as that particular variety of fish was concerned. All fishermen, from Hawaii to Niihau, observed this custom religiously. When the fishermen caught a large supply, whether by the net, hook, or shell, but one of a kind, as just stated, was reserved as an offering to Ku-ula; the remainder was then free to the people.

DEIFIED FISH SUPERSTITION

Some of the varieties of fish we now eat were deified and prayed to by the people of the olden time, and even some Hawaiians of to-day labor under like superstition with regard to sharks, eels, oopus, and some others. They are afraid to eat or touch these lest they suffer in consequence; and this belief has been perpetuated, handed down from parents to children, even to the present day. The writer was one of those brought up to this belief, and only lately has eaten the kapu fish of his ancestors without fearing a penalty therefor.

STORY OF THE ANAE-HOLO

The anae-holo is a species of mullet unlike the shallow water, or pond, variety; and the following story of its habit is well known to any *kupa* (native born) of Oahu.

The home of the anae-holo is at Honouliuli, Pearl Harbor, at a place called Ihuopalaai. They make periodical journeys around to the opposite side of the island, starting from Puuloa and going to windward, passing successively Kumumanu, Kalihi, Kou, Kalia, Waikiki, Kaalawai and so on, around to the Koolau side, ending at Laie, and then returning by the same course to their starting-point. This fish is not caught at Waianae, Kaena, Waialua, Waimea, or Kahuku because it does not run that way, though these places are well supplied with other kinds. The reason given for this is as follows:

Ihuopalaai had a Ku-ula, and this fish god supplied anaes. Ihuopalaai's sister took a husband and went and lived with him at Laie, Koolauloa. In course of time a day came when there was no fish to be had. In her distress and desire for some she bethought herself of her brother, so she sent her husband to Honouliuli to ask Ihuopalaai for a supply, saying: "Go to Ihuopalaai, my brother, and ask him for fish. If he offers you dried fish, refuse it by all means;—do not take it, because the distance is so long that you would not be able to carry enough to last us for any length of time."

When her husband arrived at Honouliuli he went to Ihuopalaai and asked him for fish. His brother-in-law gave him several large bundles of dried fish, one of which he could not very well lift, let alone carry a distance. This offer was refused and reply given

according to instruction. Ihuopalaai sat thinking for
some time and then told him to return home, saying:
"You take the road on the Kona side of the island;
do not sit, stay, nor sleep on the way till you reach
your own house."

The man started as directed, and Ihuopalaai asked
Ku-ula to send fish for his sister, and while the man
was journeying homeward as directed a school of fish
was following in the sea, within the breakers. He did
not obey fully the words of Ihuopalaai, for he became
so tired that he sat down on the way; but he noticed
that whenever he did so the fish rested too. The
people seeing the school of fish went and caught some
of them. Of course, not knowing that this was his
supply, he did not realize that the people were taking
his fish. Reaching home, he met his wife and told her
he had brought no fish, but had seen many all the
way, and pointed out to her the school of anae-holo
which was then resting abreast of their house. She
told him it was their supply, sent by Ihuopalaai, his
brother-in-law. They fished, and got all they desired,
whereupon the remainder returned by the same way
till they reached Honouliuli where Ihuopalaai was living. Ever afterward this variety of fish has come and
gone the same way every year to this day, commencing
some time in October and ending in March or April.

Expectant mothers are not allowed to eat of the
anae-holo, nor the aholehole, fearing dire consequences
to the child, hence they never touch them till after the
eventful day. Nor are these fish ever given to children
till they are able to pick and eat them of their own accord.

MYTH OF THE HILU

The hilu is said to have once possessed a human form, but by some strange event its body was changed to that of a fish. No knowledge of its ancestry or place of origin is given, but the story is as follows:

Hilu-ula and Hilu-uli were born twins, one a male and the other a female. They had human form, but with power to assume that of the fish now known as hilu. The two children grew up together and in due time when Hilu-uli, the sister, was grown up, she left her brother and parents without saying a word and went into the sea, and, assuming her fish form, set out on a journey, eventually reaching Heeia, Koolaupoko. During the time of her journey she increased the numbers of the hilu so that by the time they came close to Heeia there was so large a school that the sea was red with them. When the people of Heeia and Kaneohe saw this, they paddled out in their canoes to discover that it was a fish they had never seen nor heard of before. Returning to the shore for nets, they surrounded the school and drew in so many that they were not able to care for them in their canoes. The fishes multiplied so rapidly that when the first school was surrounded and dragged ashore, another one appeared, and so on, till the people were surfeited. Yet the fish stayed in the locality, circling around. The people ate of them in all styles known to Hawaiians; raw, lawalued, salted, and broiled over a fire of coals.

While the Koolau people were thus fishing and

feasting, Hilu-ula, the brother, arrived among them in his human form; and when he saw the hilu-uli broiling over the coal fire he recognized the fish form of his sister. This so angered him that he assumed the form of a whirlwind and entered every house where they had hilu and blew the fish all back into the sea. Since then the hilu-uli has dark scales, and is well known all over the islands.

THE HOU, OR SNORING FISH

The hou lives in shallow water. When fishing with torches on a quiet, still night, if one gets close to where it is sleeping it will be heard to snore as if it were a human being. This is a small, beautifully colored fish. Certain sharks also, sleeping in shallow water, can be heard at times indulging in the same habit.

There are many kinds of fish known to these islands, and other stories connected with them, which, if gathered together, would make an interesting collection of yarns as "fishy" as any country can produce.

THE END

GLOSSARY OF
HAWAIIAN WORDS

GLOSSARY OF HAWAIIAN WORDS

aaho, sticks for thatching, p. 142.

ahaaina, feast, p. 150.

aheahea, an edible plant, p. 135.

aholehole, a species of fish.

ahos, small sticks used in thatching, p. 245.

Ahu o Kakaalaneo, the name given to the original feather cloak, p. 155.

ahupuaa, a small division of a country under the care of a head man.

ahuula, a feather cloak, p. 155.

Ai Kanaka, man eater, p. 191.

aikane, an intimate friend of the same sex, p. 264.

Aina-i ka-kaupo-o-Kane (the land in the heart of Kane), the primeval home of mankind, p. 17.

Aina kumupuaa a Kane, see *Kanaka-maoli*.

Aina lauena a Kane, p. 24

Aina-wai-akua-a-Kane (the land of the divine water of Kane), the primeval home of mankind, p. 17.

aipuupuu, chief cook or steward, p. 141.

akaaka, laughter, p. 118.

aku, a species of fish, the bonito.

akua, a deity, p. 184.

akule, a species of fish.

ala, a smooth, round stone.

alae, mud-hens, p. 33.

alaea, red earth, of which the body of the first man was made, p. 16.

Alehe-ka-la, sun snarer, p. 32.

alii, chief.

Alii aimoku, sovereign of the land.

aloha, a word betokening greeting or farewell.

Aloha ino oe, eia ihonei paha oe e make ai, ke ai mainei Pele, Compassion great to you! Close here, perhaps, is your death; Pele comes devouring, p. 40.

Aloha oe! Alas for you! p. 41.

anaana, prayer of a Kahuna to accomplish one's death, p. 169.

anae-holo, a species of fish, p. 270.

anahulu, a period of ten days.

Ana puhi, eel's cave, p. 188.

ano akua nae, but godlike, p. 51.

Aole! no! p. 40.

ao poko, short cloud, p. 207.

apapani (or *apapane*), a scarlet bird, p. 182.

a-pe, a plant having broad leaves of an acrid taste, like kalo, but stronger.

AUK

auki, the ki leaf (*Dracœna terminalis*), p. 119.

Aumakua, ancestral shades, p. 93; god, p. 220.

aupehu, famine swollen, p. 220.

auwai, watercourse, p. 110.

Auwe ka make! alas, he is dead! p. 176.

awa, the name of a plant of a bitter, acrid taste, from which an intoxicating drink is made; also the name of the liquor itself, expressed from the root of the plant. (*Piper methysticum*).

aweoweo, a species of reddish fish.

Eia o Hana la he aina aupehu; o Hana keia i ka ia iki; ka ia o Kama; ka ia o Lanakila, p. 220.

Elepaio, a small green bird (*Chasiempis sandwichensis*), p. 125.

ha, the lower stem of leaves when cut from the root, p. 114.

haawe, back-load, p. 126.

haka, a medium devoted to the cult of a god, p. 263.

hala, tree (*Pandanus odoratissimus*), p. 121.

halau, shed, p. 113.

hau, a forest tree — a species of hibiscus.

he ekolu ula o ka la, the third brightness of the sun, p. 204.

hee kupua, wonderful octopus, p. 234.

heiau, temple.

IKI

he keehina honua a Kane, p. 15.

he'lii kahuli, a fallen chief, p. 19.

He Lualoa no Na'lii, a deep pit for the chiefs, p. 241.

he mau anahulu, several ten day periods.

He po hookahi, a ao ua pau, in one night, and by dawn it is finished, p. 109.

He waa halau Alii o ka Moku, the royal vessel, the ark, p. 20.

hiaku, name of a place in the sea beyond the kaiuli, and inside the kohola, p. 242.

Hi-ka-po-loa, a name for the godhead, p. 15.

Hilo, the first day (of the new moon), p. 75.

hilu, a species of fish, spotted with various colors, p. 273.

hinahina, leaves of a gray or withered appearance, p. 98.

hinalea, a species of wrasse-fish.

hokeo, a fisherman's gourd.

hoku kaolele, a meteor, p. 253.

holua, sled.

honu, sea turtle, p. 183.

hou, a species of fish, p. 274.

hula, a dance.

ieie, a decorative vine. (*Freyoinetia arnotti*).

iiwi, a small red bird.

i ka muli o Hea at the rear of Hea, p. 24.

Ikiki, a summer month — July or August, p. 74.

i kini akua, spirits, angels.

IKU

Ikua, a winter month — December or January, p. 74.

i kuhaia, from spittle, p. 18.

ilalo loa i ka po, deep down into darkness, p. 18.

ili hau, the bark of the hau tree from which ropes are made, p. 218.

ilio, dog.

i mea ole, as nothing.

imu, oven.

iwi kuamoo, the backbone.

ka aina i ka haupo a Kane, p. 24.

ka aina momona a Kane, the fruitful land of Kane, p. 24.

kaao, legend, p. 108.

ka holua ana o Kahawali, Kahawali's sliding-place, p. 39.

kahu, keeper, p. 188.

Kahunas, priests, p. 203.

kahuna lapaau, medical priest, p. 53.

Kaiakahinalii, the Flood, p. 20.

Kai a Kahinalii, Sea of Kahinalaa, p. 37.

kai-ula-a-Kane, the Red Sea of Kane, p. 24.

kaiuli, the deep sea.

kai waena, middle post (of a house), p. 223.

Kakelekele, hydropathic cure, p. 126.

kala, a species of fish.

Ka lae o ka ilio, the dog's forehead, p. 240.

Ka lae o ka laau, p. 240.

Kalana-i hau-ola (Kalana with the life-giving dew), the primeval home of mankind, p. 17.

KAU

kalo, the well-known vegetable of Hawaii, a species of *Arum esculentum; Colocasia antiquorum,* p. 131.

kamaainas, original inhabitants, or long residents, p. 140.

kamani tree, *Calophyllum inophyllum,* p. 72.

kanaka, a man; the general name of men, women, and children of all classes, in distinction from animals.

Kanaka-maoli, the people living on the mainland of Kane (*Aina kumupuaa a Kane*), p. 22.

Kane, sunlight, one of the three supreme gods, p. 15.

kanekoa, a deity, p. 184.

Kane-laa-uli, the fallen chief, he who fell on account of the tree, p. 17.

Kanikau, lamentation, p. 181.

ka one lauena a Kane, p. 24.

kapa, the cloth beaten from the bark of the paper mulberry, also from the bark of several other trees; hence, cloth of any kind; clothing generally.

Kapapahanaumoku, the island bearing rock or stratum, p. 49.

ka poe keokeo maoli, p. 22.

kapu, sacred.

kapu-hoano, sacred or holy days, p. 24.

kapuku, the restoration to life of the dead, p. 151.

Ka Punahou, the new spring, p. 37.

Kauakiowao, Mountain Mist, p. 133.

KAU

Kauawaahila, Waahila Rain, p. 133.

kau i ka lele, placed on the altar, p. 209.

ka-wai-ola-loa-a-Kane, water of everlasting life, p. 23.

kawelewele, guiding-ropes, p. 115.

Keakeomilu, the liver of Milu, p. 56.

keawemauhili, a deity, p. 184.

Keinohoomanawanui, a sloven, one persistently unclean, p. 88.

Ke po-lua ahi, the pit of fire, inferno, p. 18.

Ke ue nei au ia olua, I grieve for you two, p. 41.

ki, a plant having a saccharine root, the leaves of which are used for wrapping up bundles of food; the leaves are also used as food for cattle and for thatching.

kihei, a mantle worn over the shoulders.

kilu, play, or game, p. 127.

koa tree, *Acacia koa*.

ko' a aina aumakua, fishing-station, p. 229.

ko' a ia, fishing-station.

ko' a ku-ula, a temple to Kocula, p. 227.

ko' a lawaia, fishing-station, p. 222.

koali, same as *kowali*.

koas, fighting men, p. 157.

koele, a small division of land; hence, a field planted by the tenants for a landlord; a garden belonging to the chief, but cultivated by his people, p. 260.

kohola, a reef.

LAK

kolea, plover, p. 71.

kona, a severe storm that comes up from the equator, p. 183.

konane, a game like checkers.

Konohiki, feudal lord, a head man with others under him.

kou, a large shade tree growing mostly near the sea, p. 161.

kowali, convolvulus vine, a swing made of these vines, p. 46.

Ku, Substance; one of the three supreme gods.

ku, arise, stand, p. 24.

kuaha, a stone-paved platform, p. 156.

Ku-Kaua-Kahi, a triad — the Fundamental Supreme Unity, p. 15.

kukini, trained runner.

kuko, to wish, to lust, p. 89.

kukui tree, *Aleurites molluccana*, p. 88.

Kulu-ipo, the fallen chief, he who fell on account of the tree, p. 17.

kumukahi, east wind, p. 41.

Kumu-uli, the fallen tree, he who fell on account of the tree, p. 17.

kupa, native born person, p. 271.

Kupapau o Puupehe, Tomb of Puupehe, p. 181.

kupua, demigod, p. 43.

ku-ula, the fish god of Hawaiians.

Lae, cape (of land), p. 148.

la-i leaves, dracæna leaves.

laka loa, very tame, p. 216.

LAL

lalo puhaka, p. 16.

lama, a forest tree (*Maba sand-wicensis*) which has very hard wood, p. 258.

lana, floating, p. 20.

lanai, arbor, p. 150.

lau, four hundred, p. 190.

lauele, a species of turnip.

lawalu, to cook meat on the coals wrapped in ki leaves, p. 147.

leho, cowry shell.

lehoula, a species of cowry of a red color.

lehua tree, *Metrosideros polymor-pha*.

leiomano, shark's tooth weapon, p. 203.

leis, wreaths.

lele, a variety of banana, p. 150.

lelekawa, to jump from a height into deep water, p. 256.

lele kowali, swinging, p. 46.

Lelepua, arrow flight, p. 88.

lepo ula, red earth, of which the body of the first man was made, p. 16.

lilo ai kona ola a make iho la, his life was taken, so death ensued, p. 55.

limu, sea-moss, p. 242.

Lo Aikanaka, the last of the man-eating chiefs.

lomilomi, to rub or chafe the body.

Lono, Sound; one of the three Supreme gods.

lua, killing by breaking the bones, p. 142.

Lua o Milu, the nether world, p. 46.

MAN

luau, the kalo leaf; boiled herbs; young kalo leaves gathered and cooked for food.

ma, a syllable signifying accompanying, together, etc., p 54.

maika, the name of a popular game; also, the stone used for rolling in that game, p. 157.

mai ka po mai, from the time of night, darkness, chaos, p. 15.

mai, komo mai, come, come in, p. 78.

maile, *Alyxia olivaeformis*, p. 120; fine-leaved variety, *Maile laulii*, p. 95.

makaha, floodgates, p. 142.

makahelei, drawn eyes, p. 120.

makahiki, year, p. 270.

makai, seaward, p. 217.

Makakehau, Misty Eyes, p. 182.

malailua, goats without horns, such as were found on Mauna Loa, p. 24.

malau, a place in the sea where the water is still and quiet; a place where the bait for the *aku* or bonito is found, p. 246.

malos, girdles worn by the males.

mamani, or mamane (*Sophora chry-sophylla*), a hard wood tree, p. 173.

manaiaakalani, p. 218.

mana kupua, miraculous power, p. 215.

manawa ole, in no time, p. 110; in a short time, p. 113.

manienie-akiaki, a medicinal grass of the olden time, p. 135.

MAN

manini, a species of fish caught by diving, p. 250.

mano, dam, p. 110; also the general name for shark.

manohae, a ravenous shark, p. 259.

maoli, a species of banana; the long, dark-colored plantain, p. 150.

mauka, inland.

Milu, inferno.

Moi, sovereign, p. 186.

moi, a species of fish (Threadfin) of a white color.

moo, a general name for all lizards, a serpent.

Moo-kapu, sacred lands, p. 210.

mua, front; the house of a man's outfit (of several) that was Kapu to all women, even his wife, p. 258.

Na akua aumakua o ka poe kahuna kalai waa, ancestral gods of the canoe builders, p. 216.

nae, the farther side, p. 116.

na-u, jessamine, gardenia.

noa, free of, or released from Kapu, p. 135.

O haehae ka manu, ke ale nei ka wai, the water is disturbed by action of the birds, p. 95.

ohelo, a species of small reddish berry; the Hawaiian whortle-berry, p. 182.

ohia, native apple; also, a forest tree of several varieties.

ohia hemolele, the sacred apple-tree, p. 17.

PAL

ohiki-makaloa, long-eyed sand-crabs, p. 70.

ohua, the name given to the young of the *manini* fish.

Oi-e, Most Excellent, p. 15.

Oio, procession of ghosts, p. 48.

oio, a species of fish (Bonefish).

oo, digger, p. 52.

oopu, a species of small fish living in fresh water rivers and ponds.

opae, a small fish; a shrimp; a crab.

opihi-koele, a species of shell-fish, p. 224.

opihis, shell-fish, p. 70.

pa, wall, p. 157.

pa, pearl shell, p. 247.

pa hi aku, pearl fish-hook.

pahoa, stone weapon; dagger.

pahoehoe, smooth, shining lava.

pahonua, (more correctly *puuhonua*), place of refuge, p. 156.

pahoola, a remnant, a healing piece, p. 56.

pahu kaeke, a temple drum, p. 186.

paiula, the royal red kapa of old, p. 145.

pakai, an herb used for food in time of scarcity.

pakui, a house joined to a house above — that is, a tower, p. 158.

pala, ripe, soft; also, as a noun, a vegetable used as food in time of scarcity.

pale, a director, p. 115.

pali, precipice.

PAL

Pali-uli (the blue mountain), the primeval home of mankind, p. 17.

palolo, whitish clay, of which the head of the first man was made, p. 16.

pani, a stoppage, a closing up, that which stops or closes.

papa, a board; a term applied to anything of flat surface.

papa holua, a flat sled, p. 40.

pa-u, skirt.

pihoihoi loa, greatly excited, p. 206.

pili, the long, coarse grass used in thatching houses, p. 158.

pipipi, a temporary shelter hut, p. 54.

po, night, chaos, pp. 15, 49.

poe poi-uhane, spirit catchers, p. 129.

pohaku-ia, fish stone, p. 241.

poi, the paste or pudding which was formerly the chief food of the Hawaiians, and still is so to a great extent. It is made of kalo, sweet potatoes, or bread-fruit, but mostly of kalo, by baking the above articles in an underground oven, and then peeling or pounding them, adding a little water; it is then left in a mass to ferment; after fermentation, it is again worked over with more water until it has the consistency of thick paste. It is eaten cold with the fingers.

Po-ia-milu, inferno, p. 18.

UHA

Po-kini-kini, inferno, p. 18.

Po-kua-kini, inferno, p. 18.

po o akua, a certain night of the month, p. 205.

Po-papa-ia-owa, inferno, p. 18.

Po-pau-ole, endless night, p. 18.

popolo, a plant sometimes eaten in times of scarcity, also used as a medicine.

pouhana, end post (of a house).

poumanu, corner post (of a house), p. 210.

pou o manu, corner post (of a house), p. 223.

pu, head or end of a canoe, or log, on which to fasten the rope to draw it down out of the river, p. 115.

puaa, a hog, p. 16.

puhala, the hala tree, p. 233.

puhi, eel, sea snake.

puholoholo, to cook (food) by rolling with hot stones in a covered gourd, p. 135.

puloulou, sign of kapu, p. 119.

puni ka hiamoe, a trance or deep sleep, p. 81.

puoa, a burial tower, p. 148.

Reinga, the leaping place, p. 50.

tapa, see Kapa, p. 144.

Ua, rain, p. 169.

ua haki ka pule, p. 208.

ueue, bait, p. 225.

uhae ia, p. 134.

UHU

uhu, a species of fish about the size of the salmon, p. 241.

uki, a plant or shrub sometimes used in thatching; a species of grass, p. 98.

uku, a species of fish.

Ulu kapu a Kane, the breadfruit tabooed for Kane, p. 17.

uo, a part of the process of feather cloak making, p. 155.

uwau, a species of bird; a kind of waterfowl.

waa, canoe, p. 194.

waa halau, see *He waa halau Alii o ka Moku.*

WIL

Wai a Hiku, water of Hiku, p. 44.

Waiakoloa, p. 192.

Wai nao, spittle, p. 16.

waoke, or wauke, (*Broussonetia papyrifera*), the plant furnishing bark for the best Kapa, p.79.

Wawa ka Menehune i Puukapele, ma Kauai, puohu ka manu o ka loko o Kawainui ma Koolaupoko, Oahu, the hum of the voices of the Menehunes at Puukapele, Kauai, startled the birds of the pond of Kawainui, at Koolaupoko, Oahu, p. 111.

wiliwili tree, *Erythrina monosperma,* p. 121.

TALES OF THE PACIFIC

JACK LONDON
Stories of Hawaii $6.95
South Sea Tales $6.95

HAWAII
Ancient History of the Hawaiian People to the Times of Kamehameha I $7.95
Remember Pearl Harbor by Blake Clark $4.95
Kona by Marjorie Sinclair $6.95
A Hawaiian Reader $6.95
A Hawaiian Reader, Vol. II $6.95
Teller of Hawaiian Tales by Eric Knudsn $6.95
Myths and Legends of Hawaii by W.D. Westervelt $5.95
Mark Twain in Hawaii $4.95
The Legends and Myths of Hawaii by Kalakaua $7.95
Hawaii's Story by Hawaii's Queen $7.95
Rape in Paradise by Theon Wright $5.95
The Betrayal of Liliuokalani $7.95
The Wild Wind by Marjorie Sinclair $6.95

SOUTH SEAS LITERATURE
The Lure of Tahiti ed. by A. Grove Day $5.95
The Blue of Capricorn by Eugene Burdick $5.95
Horror in Paradise, ed. by A. Grove Day and Bacil F. Kirtley $6.95
Best South Sea Stories, ed. by A. Grove Day $6.95

TRAVEL, BIOGRAPHY, ANTHROPOLOGY
Home from the Sea: Robert Louis Stevenson in Samoa, by Richard Bermann $5.95
The Nordhoff-Hall Story: In Search of Paradise by Paul L. Briand $5.95
A Dream of Islands by Gavan Daws $4.95
Kalakaua: Renaissance King $6.95
Nahi'ena'ena: Sacred Daughter of Hawai'i $4.95
Around the World With a King $5.95

Orders should be sent to Mutual Publishing Co.
1215 Center Street, Suite 210, Honolulu, HI 96816.
For book rate shipping, add $3.00 for first book, $1.00 for each additional book (4-6 weeks; in Hawaii, 1-2 weeks); for first class, add $4.00 for first book, $3.00 for each additional book (1-2 weeks).